CHILDREN WORSHIP!

MaryJane Pierce Norton

DISCIPLESHIP RESOURCES

P O BOX 340003 • NASHVILLE, TN 37203-0003
www.discipleshipresources.org

Third printing: 2008

Library of Congress Card Catalog No. 97-66575

ISBN # 978-0-88177-223-4

DR223

Table of Contents

Introduction 4

Section 1
Planning Guide 7

    Checklist for Planning 8

    Teacher Training Session 11

    The Children We Teach 14

    Multiple Intelligences 17

    For the Pastor 18

    Session-by-Session Suggestions for Worship 19

Section 2
Bulletin Inserts 25

Section 3
Letters to the Parents 35

Section 4
Session Plans 53

    Session One: WE GATHER TO WORSHIP 54

    Session Two: WE GATHER TO WORSHIP 61

    Session Three: WE PRAISE AND THANK GOD 68

    Session Four: WE PRAISE AND THANK GOD 73

    Session Five: WE PRAY 78

    Session Six: WE PRAY 83

    Session Seven: WE PROCLAIM GOD'S WORD 89

    Session Eight: WE PROCLAIM GOD'S WORD 95

    Session Nine: WE PROCLAIM GOD'S WORD 99

    Session Ten: WE RESPOND TO GOD'S CALL 106

    Session Eleven: WE RESPOND TO GOD'S CALL 111

    Session Twelve: WE ARE SENT INTO THE WORLD 117

    Session Thirteen: WE WORSHIP GOD! 123

Evaluation 128

Introduction

Sometimes it is a short fall from the theoretical to the practical.

A professor-friend of mine, a staunch advocate for involving children in worship, believes that all people of the family of God should be a part of the gathered community of worship. He believes that children are full contributors to the worship experience. He believes that children bring unique gifts of wonder, excitement, and creativity that make worship more meaningful for adults. He still believes this, even after several challenging worship services with his kindergarten-aged daughter in tow!

Children from his congregation normally did not attend morning worship services until they reached kindergarten age. My friend looked forward to the time when he would be able to enjoy having his child with him during worship. It was not quite what he expected.

Oh, there was excitement. But it stemmed from dropped markers rolling hither and yon on the floor. Oh, there was freshness. But it came from a five-year-old who "whispered" her questions so loudly that they carried all the way to the front of the church. Oh, there was joy. But the joy of discovery sometimes happened during silent prayer. In his words, "I left worship exhausted, asking myself, 'Will I ever be able to worship with my child beside me?'"

His experience is not unique. What happens when children with wiggling bodies, loud voices, and lots of questions enter worship? How do we help children appreciate and participate in worship without losing the excitement and awe they so readily bring? What are the "manners" for worship that enable children to successfully participate in worship without fear of frowns, head shakes, finger snaps, and laughs at their mistakes?

Try an experiment. Walk up to a group of adults in your congregation and say, "Children in worship." You may hear parents say, "Great idea. Do you want to sit with mine?" You may hear other adults say, "Aren't they cute. Now why can't they be quiet and still?" You may hear pastors say, "I know they should be here, but they distract me from what I'm trying to get across to adults." You may hear children say, "It's boring. I'd rather be in the nursery."

And yet, how can we pass the faith from generation to generation if all of us are not there as a part of God's family? Children belong in worship. But sometimes it helps to have planned experiences that enable them to know what is expected, how to participate, and what our words and actions mean. For this reason, *Children Worship!* was created.

Who Is This For?

Children Worship! is designed as a worship education class experience for children, ages five to eight, or as an intergenerational study for children, their families, and other adults who want to encourage young people to participate in worship. It contains material that can appear in church newsletters and bulletins for the benefit of all members of the congregation. It contains information that explains to parents what their children are studying from session to session, and it makes suggestions for reinforcing those learnings at home. It also includes session-by-session suggestions for pastors to use in worship.

What Is Its Purpose?

The purpose of this study is to help children and adults strengthen their participation in congregational worship. Adults and children should come away from this study with a greater understanding of what worship offers to all, regardless of age, and its relationship to God. As children understand what we do in worship, they can participate more fully, and adults can learn from the children.

When Should It Be Used?

Children Worship! is designed to be used in a variety of settings and times. The thirteen-session study should follow a regular schedule, with as little time as possible between sessions. Depending on what suits your church, you may decide to combine the sessions into two-hour classes, which would complete the course in seven sessions instead of thirteen. In most cases there are two sessions related to each movement of worship, so expect some duplication of activities, Scripture, and objectives. Since children learn through repetition, the recurring elements in the sessions are designed to reinforce what is being taught.

Children Worship! can be used as a program for afterschool hours, for Sunday mornings, afternoons, or evenings, or even for a weekend retreat. Change and adapt the material so that it works in the way that is best for your congregation.

What Is Contained in This Manual?

In this manual you will find:

- Material for thirteen sessions, each lasting forty-five to sixty minutes, including activity sheets that can be duplicated and used in the session.
- Bulletin inserts that can be duplicated to help the congregation know what the participants are learning.
- Letters that can be duplicated and sent to parents to help them reinforce what is being done in each session.
- Worship suggestions for use during the time children are involved in the study.
- Suggestions for a church-wide study on children and worship.

What Is the Recipe for Success?

Take this manual, mix it with leaders who care for children and who believe in the importance of worship. Add clergy and staff who support faith formation and who see worship as an important place where faith is formed. Include parents committed to helping their children be present for the sessions and to working with the material at home. Do not forget children who are eager to learn. And pray for God's presence, blessing, and guidance in this journey of faith and discovery about worship.

Section 1

Planning Guide

Checklist for Planning

Three to Four Months Before the Study

Make decisions
- [ ] Date to begin the study
- [ ] Time of day or evening for the study
- [ ] Ages of the children
- [ ] Intergenerational study, congregational study, or children-only study
- [ ] Location of the study

Estimate number of students
- [ ] Plan for one adult per six to eight children. (If parents or other adults will be participating with the children, you will not need as many leaders.)

Preview manual
- [ ] Order a manual for each leader.

Receive approval
- [ ] Ask the appropriate governing board in your church to approve the study.
- [ ] Ask for approval to include bulletin inserts in the weekly bulletin during the study.

Two to Three Months Before the Study

Recruit leaders
- [ ] Sunday school teachers
- [ ] Parents of children
- [ ] Worship committee members
- [ ] Vacation Bible school teachers
- [ ] Church staff
- [ ] Retired people
- [ ] Young adults or older youth

Publicize
- [ ] Letter to parents
- [ ] Article in church newsletter
- [ ] Announcement in worship

Plan training
- [ ] Set meeting dates for leaders and church staff.
- [ ] Plan training session to help adults become familiar with manual.
- [ ] Discuss length of study, beginning and ending dates.

Two to Six Weeks Before the Study

Hold training
- [ ] Distribute manuals.
- [ ] Plan first session together.
- [ ] Put together a list of needed resources.
- [ ] Check space to be used for the sessions.
- [ ] Explain procedures for purchasing or acquiring supplies.

Publicize
- [ ] Second letter to parents
- [ ] Second article in church newsletter
- [ ] Second announcement in worship

One Week Before the Study

Check and make ready
- [ ] Each leader has manual
- [ ] Materials duplicated
- [ ] Supplies, equipment
- [ ] Room
- [ ] Dedication of leaders and participants in worship

During the Study
- [ ] Weekly evaluation
- [ ] Plan for next session.
- [ ] Check supplies.
- [ ] Ready materials for duplication.
- [ ] Keep accurate records of attendance, finances, and so forth.

☐ Recruit substitutes, as needed.
☐ Recruit special speakers, as needed.
☐ Place progress reports in church newsletter or bulletin.

As the Study Ends
☐ Celebration during worship
☐ Thanks to all adult leaders and teachers

One to Two Weeks Later
Evaluate
☐ Note suggestions for next year's study.
☐ File all records.
☐ Prepare follow-up report for church newsletter or bulletin.

Using This Study Intergenerationally

Children Worship! is designed as a study for a group consisting of children, youth, and adults. *Children Worship!* can be used as a study for children only or as a congregational study. As people of all ages learn about worship together, the congregation can be strengthened in its appreciation of how each person contributes to worship.

A class consisting of up to twenty-four participants is manageable. Consider dividing a class of more than twenty-four into smaller "church family" groups. Divide the classes into a good mix of children, youth, and adults. Recruit separate leaders for each church family group. Run the sessions simultaneously but have separate classroom space for each.

Planning Notes

We Need Leaders!!!

Where do you get leaders for this study? How do you train them? As you plan to recruit leaders, consider the following potential sources:

- *Parents of children who will be in the study:* Some parents would welcome the chance to learn more about worship with their children.
- *People who are currently serving, or have previously served, on the worship committee:* Many who serve on this committee have a deep commitment to worship and want to see others enjoy and benefit from the services. Some may be willing to work with others who have experience working with children.
- *Older youth or young adults:* While some in this group may not be ready for sole leadership, they may be willing to lend a helping hand.
- *People who have previously taught children but who are not currently teaching:* Since this study has only thirteen sessions, those who do not want to volunteer for a long-term weekly responsibility may be willing to lead for this short time.
- *People who love and understand children.*
- *People who serve as worship leaders:* Talking with and getting to know those who lead during services will help children be more involved when they are in worship.

Top Ten List of Recruiting Leaders

1. Be realistic about the time commitment required. Good leaders always prepare, and that takes time. Careful and thorough planning leads to good sessions.
2. Recruit enough teachers. When a group has children of various ages, several adults are needed to ensure success and to prevent accidents and chaos.
3. Approach potential leaders with a positive attitude. Negative approaches ("I'm sure you don't have time to do this, but I'll ask anyway.") usually produce negative responses.
4. Emphasize the importance of the study. Statements that downplay the significance ("It's only an hour so; anyone can keep children occupied for that long.") may lead adults to feel that the study is not worth their time.
5. Promise leaders the help they need to get started. Continue to support them throughout the study.
6. Explain the importance of studying worship and the benefits that will come to all participants of the study.
7. Offer training throughout the study.
8. Provide the necessary supplies and materials to ensure good sessions.
9. Explain the prayer support and congregational support they will receive during the study.
10. Recognize their gifts and graces, and explain how you see these as important for leading this study.

Teacher Training Session

Now that you have recruited the leaders, it is time to think about what you will do to train them. The following plan will work in a two-hour training experience. You can adjust the time up to two and a half hours, depending on the needs of the team.

Training Design

Purpose
To prepare leaders for *Children Worship!*

Supplies
- *Children Worship!* manuals
- copies of "Scavenger Hunt for Leaders" (p. 13)
- Bibles
- Hymnals
- Markers and pencils
- Newsprint
- Balloons (real or cutouts from construction paper)
- Elastic
- Jingle bells
- Needles and thread
- Paper towel cardboard tubes
- Wax paper
- Rubber bands
- Nametags in red, green, orange, and yellow
- worship table with candles, a cross, and flowers

Explain the Purpose of the Training (10 minutes)
Invite each participant to make a nametag using the markers and the church-shaped cutouts. After they have finished, invite them to join you in a circle around the worship table. Sing together, "This Is the Day" (No. 657 in *The United Methodist Hymnal*). Inform the participants that they are preparing to teach *Children Worship!* by
- learning about the children they will teach.
- exploring the teaching manual.
- experiencing some of the activities found in Session One.

Review "The Children We Teach" (15 minutes)
Lead the participants in a discussion about what to expect from the children in the class. Use the material found in the section "The Children We Teach" (p. 14) and "Multiple Intelligences" (p. 17). Provide specific information about the children—names, ages, readers or non-readers, and so forth.

Explore the Manual (30 minutes)
Distribute the manuals to the participants. Divide the group into four teams by asking participants to gather with those who have nametags of the same color. (If you have a small group, you may want to work as one team or divide into fewer teams.)

Say: "For the next twenty minutes you're going to explore the manual through a scavenger hunt. I'll give you a checklist. All of the items can be found in the manual. You may want to divide the items among your team members or you may want to work together to find each item. It's up to you to decide." Distribute copies of "Scavenger Hunt for Leaders" (p. 13).

Call time at the end of twenty minutes. Encourage those who found all of the items to tell where they found them and to give their answers to the questions. Answer any questions they have related to the use of the manual. Remind them that there will be some duplication in the sessions (especially those related to the movements of worship).

Explain the teacher's role in gathering supplies, purchasing materials, or recruiting other helpers.

Break (5 minutes)

Experience Activities from Session One (30 to 40 minutes)
Call the group back together. Explain that they will now experience some of the activities found in Session One. Invite them to participate as if they were children coming to the first session.

Give each participant a balloon or a balloon cutout. Ask them to draw or write on the balloon something they do when they are in worship with their family. When all are finished, sit in a circle and let each one describe what they have drawn.

Read or tell the story of Jesus going to the synagogue (Luke 4:16-21). Talk about how this was a time for Jesus to go to church. Explain that when we come together with others who believe in God, we are in worship. Tell them that we will be learning about why we do what

we do in worship over the next few weeks. Ask if they have questions about what we do in worship. Say that you will not answer all of their questions today, but you will write them on newsprint so that they can be answered as we study together.

Tell the group that the Psalms help us to see worship in many different forms. Read Psalm 98:4-6. Ask the group about the way people were encouraged to show joy in this passage. Explain that playing instruments in church shows joy. Show the group where the materials are for making a horn or a set of wrist bells. Invite each to choose an instrument to make.

When all have completed their instruments, call the group back together. Sing "This Is the Day," using the instruments to accompany the singing.

Gather around the worship table. Read Psalm 46:10. Ask the group to think of quiet times during worship. Have a time of silence, then pray together, asking God to be with you as you lead this study.

Wrap-up and Evaluation (10 minutes)
Answer any questions that participants may have about teaching. Ask for oral evaluations of the leadership training. Dismiss with prayer.

Scavenger Hunt for Leaders

Use your manual and locate the following information:

1. Find the session containing a Scripture reference from Luke. What is the reference? In what session do you find the reference?

_____

_____

_____

_____

2. Find the place in the lesson plan that calls for worship. Note where it appears in every session.

_____

_____

_____

_____

3. Find the activity that tells about the *Gloria Patri*. What do these words mean?

_____

_____

_____

_____

4. Find the place in the lesson plan that lets you know what supplies are needed. Make note of one or two of the more unusual supply needs.

_____

_____

_____

_____

5. Find the place within the manual that mentions the length of the sessions.

_____

_____

_____

_____

6. Find the session containing the explanation of baptism. List items you may have at home that you could use in this session.

_____

_____

_____

_____

7. Find the place in the lesson plan that cites what Scriptures to use. Pick one Scripture that seems intriguing to you.

_____

_____

_____

_____

8. Find the session that deals with the benediction and dismissal. Write a common benediction used in your congregation.

_____

_____

_____

_____

9. Find the session where the song "This Is the Day" is suggested. List another hymn or song you would like to teach to the children during this study.

_____

_____

_____

_____

10. Find the session pertaining to the seasons of the church year. List the seasons and the colors used for each one.

_____

_____

_____

_____

The Children We Teach

This study is designed to be used most successfully with children between the ages of five and eight years. It can be done with children alone or as an intergenerational program for children and their parents or other faith mentors. In most churches, children who have entered kindergarten have graduated from preschool care during worship. In many churches they are now expected to participate in worship. While we recognize that children at every age are open to God and are able to participate in worship, there are advantages to teaching the habits and skills of worship to them. Our teaching is enhanced when we know something about the behaviors, abilities, and preferences of this age group.

For every description written about children of a particular age, there is probably an exception to that description. Children in any given group provide a picture of varying abilities, varying ways of relating to peers and to adults, varying interests, and varying appearances. Thus, sometimes, things we cannot expect will happen. On the other hand, there are some predictors of behavior based on developmental theory. For those who work with children, knowing some of the expected behaviors can provide good information for planning sessions with children.

Five- and Six-Year Olds

Five- and six-year olds are at an in-between stage. Some days, their play is like that of preschoolers. They are drawn to playacting the events of the home environment. Other days, they seek to mimic older children by playing card games, by turning up their noses at anything they label as for babies, and by drawing detailed pictures of scenes imagined and real. They are seeking to succeed in a school environment and often enjoy practicing their new writing and reading skills. However, at other times, they will refuse to do these same activities, saying, "You know I can't read yet. I'm only five."

Five- and six-year-olds like group activities, but they always want to be first. They can wait patiently for turns if they are assured that their turn will come. These turns, though, must come within the same session. Taking turns from week to week does not satisfy their need for participation.

Five- and six-year-olds have best friends, but these change frequently with apparent ease. Boys and girls still play together, although more distinctions between boy activities and girl activities will appear.

Five- and six-year-olds are eager to learn, but they become frustrated because their physical ability still has not caught up with their urge to do more complicated tasks. They will want to do an activity's scissor-work themselves. But, if it takes too long, they will become tired and ask for help. Constant movement and activity are part of being five and six.

The teacher is very important to five- and six-year-olds, many times more important than their parents and (most of the time) their age peers. Older peers, however, are very appealing to five- and six-year-olds. They will do something willingly if it is suggested by an older child—something they might not do otherwise if suggested by a child their own age or by an adult.

Many five- and six-year-olds remain self centered. However, they are beginning to move to an awareness of others, and they are capable of reflecting on the needs of others, especially if these needs are related to needs of their own. Five- and six-year-olds need adults who are willing to show affection, to praise their efforts, and to encourage them in tasks that may seem too hard. They need times to be active and times to be quiet. They need many smaller group experiences where they can receive the much-wanted teacher input and yet can build toward larger group experiences. Five- and six-year-olds need adults who will share their faith, model prayer and praise, and provide a Christian witness through their actions. They also need adults who will offer opportunities for the child to express his or her own faith without demanding explanations or understandings of these faith expressions.

Seven- and Eight-Year-Olds

Because many children do not begin kindergarten until they are six, many children who have completed first grade are nearer age eight than age seven. Children in the same grade will vary in size and ability. These children are the true younger elementary students—in the early grades of school and still struggling with skills related to reading and writing.

Seven- and eight-year-old boys and girls have grown more in their awareness of others. They are becoming more ethical, with an emphasis on being fair. A common cry of a child of this age is, "It just isn't fair." They look at the fairness of every situation—from how many snacks they get to why a tornado hit a town.

Seven- and eight-year-olds have difficulty sensing shades of behavior. From their view, if something is good, then it is purely good; if something is bad, then it is purely bad. It is difficult helping them see how things that have happened in their church, in their school, or in their community can be a mixture of bad and good.

Seven- and eight-year-olds can be very steadfast in their opinions. Even when another child or an adult provides proof that what the child is saying is incorrect, the child may refuse to budge from his or her opinion. In working with this age and in asking their opinions, adults will need to work hard to help the children listen to one another and to accept another view without making judging statements.

Younger elementary children are becoming increasingly more skilled at using their hands and at eye-hand coordination. They can do more complicated art, and they are developing a stronger drive for perfection.

Adults are important to the younger elementary children. More and more, they see themselves as separate from their families, but they still identify with significant adults.

They form more lasting friendships, and some of these may last for years.

Self-expression for the early elementary child is still experimental and full of discovery as the child finds what he or she can do with words, with art, with music, and with dance. Self-discovery abounds as the child experiments with many forms of expression before finding what means most to him or her.

Younger elementary children like responsibility, and they will gladly volunteer for tasks. However, they need guidance since they are not quite ready for self-governance.

Younger elementary children are doers and are in constant motion. In group situations you will see scuffling, chasing, and moving. This age enjoys acting out and dramatizing, but they need guidance because they are not always able to think of their own ideas.

Seven- and eight-year-olds are avid collectors of things like rocks, sticks, and other seemingly insignificant (at least to the adult mind) things. This love for personal collections sometimes can generate fights of "what's fair and what's mine" within a group.

Younger elementary children need adults who understand their energy and their need for movement. They need adults who are able to spell out the rules and help them stay within the boundaries set for the group. They need adults who will introduce many ways for them to express their feelings and their faith. Adults working with this age need to realize that sticking to a project may be difficult. Providing checkpoints along the way and breaking a project into smaller parts can help the boys and girls complete tasks. While seven- and eight-year-olds may be more able to express their faith, they may also be more shy in volunteering their feelings about God and about the church. They respond to adults who talk about and willingly express themselves in prayer and in praise to God.

Multiple Intelligences

What This Means for Planning

Did you ever take an IQ test? These tests are supposed to measure a person's intelligence quotient—the ability of the person to learn and to use what is learned. While in the past we might have referred to intelligence as if it were a single item, we now know that there are multiple intelligences. In recent years there has been considerable attention given to helping children learn by planning for the different intelligences in people. We highlight this learning theory because it helps us recognize an important fact about learning. Human beings have many forms of gaining information and turning that information into knowledge. Some people are stronger at one mode of intelligence than at another. Therefore, if we plan activities within a session that lean on the strengths of as many of these intelligences as possible, children are more likely to learn. Remember, our goal is that children grow in faith as they learn about worship. We are nurturing their spiritual growth as well as their physical and mental growth when we use knowledge about multiple intelligences. In each session of *Children Worship!* activities are included that will use the intelligences listed below.

Musical
The ability to produce and to recognize songs. This is nurtured through singing, listening to music, and playing musical instruments.

Logical/mathematical
The ability to understand numbers, sequence, cause and effect, patterns, and predictability. This is nurtured through the use of manipulatives and symbols.

Interpersonal
The ability to understand and to work with others. This is nurtured through discussion, problem solving, and playing games.

Intrapersonal
The ability to understand oneself, how one is similar to and different from others. This is nurtured in encouraging children to express their own emotions, ideas, and preferences.

Bodily/kinesthetic
The ability to use the body for making things or moving in dance or in sports. This is nurtured by providing activities that exercise both the small muscles (like those used in cutting or drawing) and the large muscles (like those used in movement and in signing).

Linguistic
The ability to use language, learn words, and tell stories. This is nurtured through writing, reading, and talking about experiences.

Spatial
The ability to form a mental image of the ways things exist in space. This is nurtured in exploring buildings, mapping the location of items in a room, painting, building models, and arranging materials in space (such as flowers in a vase).

For more information about multiple intelligences, read *Frames of Mind, The Theory of Multiple Intelligences* by Howard Gardner (New York: Basic Books, 1983).

For the Pastor

Teacher

As the pastor of the congregation, you may wish to be counted among the teachers in the weekly sessions of *Children Worship!* Being a teacher for this study offers many positive opportunities:

- As pastor, you are available each week to answer questions as they occur in the sessions.
- Both children and adults benefit from being able to relate to their pastor in a setting other than formal worship.
- In any congregation, the involvement of the pastor often signals to members that the activity is important. Those who might be reluctant at first to enter the study might be persuaded to participate by your involvement.

For the pastor to be involved, the sessions of *Children Worship!* will most likely need to be held at a time other than Sunday morning. This will need to be considered when setting up the schedule for the sessions.

Supporter

While the pastor may be unable to serve as a teacher for *Children Worship!*, he or she can be a supporter of and advocate for the study by:

- intentionally praying for those who are teaching and those who are participating in the sessions, both individually and corporately, during worship services during the study.
- including the provided weekly inserts in the Sunday bulletin as the study progresses.
- beginning the study with the litany included in the bulletin inserts.
- including participants in worship leadership at the end of the study.
- leading the congregation in celebrating and blessing those who have completed the study.
- including music, Scripture, and prayers suggested for each session in the worship services.

Session-by-Session Worship Suggestions

Included in this chart is the focus for each session, the Scripture and hymns used in the sessions (as well as other related hymns), and the prayers recommended for worship during the study. *Children Worship!* focuses on the movements of worship: the gathering, praise and thanksgiving, praying, proclaiming, responding, and sending. There are two sessions for most movements. Three sessions focus on proclamation, and one session focuses on sending. The final session serves as a review and can be a time for participants to prepare to take part in congregational worship. Hymns marked with an asterisk (*) are those used in the sessions. All hymns and prayers are from *The United Methodist Book of Worship* or *The United Methodist Hymnal*.

Session	Focus	Scripture in the Session	Suggested Hymns	Suggested Prayers
Session One: We Gather to Worship	God's grace calls us together in community. God's people come together in praise and worship of God.	Luke 4:16-21 (Jesus worshiped regularly.)	*"This Is the Day" (No. 657 in *The United Methodist Hymnal*)	"This is the day that the Lord has made" (No. 450 in *The United Methodist Book of Worship*)
		Psalm 98:4-6 (Corporate worship is a joyous, celebrative time.)	"Here, O Lord, Your Servants Gather" (No. 552 in *The United Methodist Hymnal*)	"God our Mother and Father" (No. 466 in *The United Methodist Book of Worship*)
		Psalm 46:10 (Worship is sometimes quiet and personal.)	"Lift High the Cross" (No. 159 in *The United Methodist Hymnal*)	"Psalm 84" (No. 804 in *The United Methodist Hymnal*)
		1 John 4:19 (We love because God first loved us.)	"We Gather Together" (No. 131 in *The United Methodist Hymnal*)	
Session Two: We Gather to Worship	God's grace calls us together in community. God's people come together in praise and worship of God.	Psalm 95:1-7a (God's people are called to worship God, to sing unto God, and to praise God the Creator.)	*"This Is the Day" (No. 657 in *The United Methodist Hymnal*)	"Psalm 95" (No. 814 in *The United Methodist Hymnal*)
		Luke 2:41-52 (Jesus visited the Temple.)	"Come, We That Love the Lord" (No. 732 in *The United Methodist Hymnal*)	"New every morning is your love" (No. 877 in *The United Methodist Hymnal*)
		Psalm 122:1 (I was glad when I was invited to God's house.)	"Jesus, We Want to Meet" (No. 661 in *The United Methodist Hymnal*)	"In the midst of the congregation I will praise you" (No. 451 in *The United Methodist Book of Worship*)
			"All Hail the Power of Jesus' Name" (No. 154 in *The United Methodist Hymnal*)	"For Help for the Forthcoming Day" (No. 681 in *The United Methodist Hymnal*)

Session	Focus	Scripture in the Session	Suggested Hymns	Suggested Prayers
Session Three: We Praise and Thank God	God's grace moves us to praise and gratitude. We praise and thank God.	Psalm 98:4-6 (Make a joyous noise to God.)	*"Come, Christians, Join to Sing" (No. 158 in *The United Methodist Hymnal*) "Holy God, We Praise Thy Name" (No. 79 in *The United Methodist Hymnal*) "Praise to the Lord, the Almighty" (No. 139 in *The United Methodist Hymnal*) "Now Thank We All Our God" (No. 102 in *The United Methodist Hymnal*)	"Thank you, Creator of the universe" (No. 558 in *The United Methodist Book of Worship*) "Almighty God, giver of every good and perfect gift" (No. 555 in *The United Methodist Book of Worship*) "Psalm 146" (No. 858 in *The United Methodist Hymnal*)
Session Four: We Praise and Thank God	God's grace moves us to praise and gratitude. We praise and thank God.	Psalm 98:4-6 (It is good to praise God with song.) Psalm 104:33-34 (I will praise God with song all my life.)	*"Come, Christians, Join to Sing" (No. 158 in *The United Methodist Hymnal*) "For the Beauty of the Earth" (No. 92 in *The United Methodist Hymnal*) "God of the Sparrow, God of the Whale" (No. 122 in *The United Methodist Hymnal*) "We Gather Together" (No. 131 in *The United Methodist Hymnal*)	"O God, our Guide and Guardian" (No. 460 in *The United Methodist Book of Worship*) "For a New Day" (No. 676 in *The United Methodist Hymnal*) "Psalm 148" (No. 861 in *The United Methodist Hymnal*)
Session Five: We Pray	God's grace prompts our prayers. God's people speak and listen to God through prayer at church and in daily life.	Matthew 6:5-13 (Jesus teaches his disciples to pray.)	*"It's Me, It's Me, O Lord" (No. 352 in *The United Methodist Hymnal*) "My Prayer Rises to Heaven (No. 498 in *The United Methodist Hymnal*) "Sweet Hour of Prayer" (No. 395 in *The United Methodist Hymnal*)	The Lord's Prayer "The Collect" (No. 447 in *The United Methodist Book of Worship*) "O Lord our God" (No. 467 in *The United Methodist Book of Worship*) "Psalm 70" (No. 793 in *The United Methodist Hymnal*)

Children Worship!

Session	Focus	Scripture in the Session	Suggested Hymns	Suggested Prayers
Session Six: We Pray	God's grace prompts our prayers. God's people speak and listen to God through prayer at church and in daily life.	Psalm 9:1-2 (God's people are to give thanks to God whole-heartedly.) 1 Thessalonians 5:16-18 (God's people are encouraged to pray at all times.)	*"It's Me, It's Me, O Lord" (No. 352 in *The United Methodist Hymnal*) "Every Time I Feel the Spirit" (No. 404 in *The United Methodist Hymnal*) "Take Time to Be Holy" (No. 395 in *The United Methodist Hymnal*) "Jesus, Remember Me" (No. 488 in *The United Methodist Hymnal*)	The Lord's Prayer "Three Things We Pray" (No. 493 in *The United Methodist Hymnal*) "The Prayer of Saint Francis" (No. 481 in *The United Methodist Hymnal*) "Psalm 4" (No. 741 in *The United Methodist Hymnal*)
Session Seven: We Proclaim God's Word	God gives us God's Word. We listen for God's Word, and we proclaim God's Word to others.	Samuel 3:1-10 (God calls to Samuel and Samuel listened to God.) Psalm 23 (God will care for us.) Luke 18:15-17 (Jesus includes children.)	*"Tell Me the Stories of Jesus" (No. 277 in *The United Methodist Hymnal*) "Thy Word Is a Lamp" (No. 601 in *The United Methodist Hymnal*) "Come! Come! Everybody Worship" (No. 199 in *The United Methodist Book of Worship*)	"Concerning the Scripture" (No. 602 in *The United Methodist Hymnal*) "Whether the Word Be Preached or Read" (No. 595 in *The United Methodist Hymnal*) "Psalm 143:1-10" (No. 856 in *The United Methodist Hymnal*)
Session Eight: We Proclaim God's Word	God gives us God's Word. We listen for God's Word, and we proclaim God's Word to others.	Colossians 1:28 (We are to proclaim Christ.) Acts 3:11-26 (Peter preaches.)	*"Tell Me the Stories of Jesus" (No. 277 in *The United Methodist Hymnal*) "Blessed Jesus, at Thy Word" (No. 596 in *The United Methodist Hymnal*) "Wonderful Words of Life" (No. 600 in *The United Methodist Hymnal*)	"Come, Divine Interpreter" (No. 594 in *The United Methodist Hymnal*) "For the Spirit of Truth" (No. 597 in *The United Methodist Hymnal*) "Psalm 132:1-5, 11-18" (No. 849 in *The United Methodist Hymnal*)

Session	Focus	Scripture in the Session	Suggested Hymns	Suggested Prayers
Session Nine: We Proclaim God's Word	God gives us God's Word. We listen for God's Word, and we proclaim God's Word to others.	Luke 1:39-56 (Mary prepares for Jesus' birth.) Luke 2:1-20 (Jesus' birth) Matthew 2:1-12 (The Magi visit Jesus.) Matthew 27:27-50 (Jesus' death) Matthew 28 (Jesus' resurrection) Acts 2:1-4 (Pentecost) Matthew 18:1-5 (Jesus teaches.)	*"Tell Me the Stories of Jesus" (No. 277 in *The United Methodist Hymnal*) "Prepare the Way of the Lord" (No. 207 in *The United Methodist Hymnal*) "On Eagle's Wings" (No. 143 in *The United Methodist Hymnal*) "Spirit Song" (No. 347 in *The United Methodist Hymnal*)	"Everlasting God, the radiance of faithful souls" (No. 297 in *The United Methodist Book of Worship*) "Prayer to the Holy Spirit" (No. 329 in *The United Methodist Hymnal*) "Psalm 48" (No. 782 in *The United Methodist Hymnal*)
Session Ten: We Respond to God's Call	God's grace prompts us to respond to God's love. We hear and respond to God's call in our lives.	Mark 1:9-11 (Jesus is baptized.) Acts 8:12-13 (Believers are baptized.) Acts 16:11-15 (Lydia is baptized.)	*"This Little Light of Mine" (No. 585 in *The United Methodist Hymnal*) *"Here I Am, Lord" (No. 593 in *The United Methodist Hymnal*) "Child of Blessing, Child of Promise" (No. 611 in *The United Methodist Hymnal*) "You Have Put On Christ" (No. 609 in *The United Methodist Hymnal*)	"A Covenant Prayer in the Wesleyan Tradition" (No. 607 in *The United Methodist Hymnal*) "For God's Gifts" (No. 489 in *The United Methodist Hymnal*) "Psalm 100" (No. 821 in *The United Methodist Hymnal*)
Session Eleven: We Respond to God's Call	God's grace prompts us to respond to God's love. We hear and respond to God's call in our lives.	Exodus 12:1-20 (The story of the Passover) Matthew 26:26-29, Mark 14:22-25, and Luke 22:12-20 (Accounts of the Last Supper) 1 Corinthians 11:23-26 (The gathering of the early church to celebrate Communion)	*"This Little Light of Mine" (No. 585 in *The United Methodist Hymnal*) *"Let Us Break Bread Together" (No. 618 in *The United Methodist Hymnal*) *"Here I am Lord" (No. 593 in *The United Methodist Hymnal*) "Come, Let Us Eat" (No. 625 in *The United Methodist Hymnal*) "You Satisfy the Hungry Heart" (No. 629 in *The United Methodist Hymnal*)	"Bread and Justice" (No. 639 in *The United Methodist Hymnal*) "Prayer of John Chrysostom" (No. 412 in *The United Methodist Hymnal*) "For Holiness of Heart" (No. 401 in *The United Methodist Hymnal*) "Psalm 17:1-7, 15" (No. 749 in *The United Methodist Hymnal*)

Children Worship!

Session	Focus	Scripture in the Session	Suggested Hymns	Suggested Prayers
Session Twelve: We Are Sent into the World	God sends us into the world. We go from worship into the world to love God and our neighbors.	Matthew 28:18-20 (The Great Commission)	*"Here I Am, Lord" (No. 593 in *The United Methodist Hymnal*) *"Go Now in Peace" (No. 665 in *The United Methodist Hymnal*) "Sent Forth by God's Blessing" (No. 664 in *The United Methodist Hymnal*) "Lead Me, Lord" (No. 473 in *The United Methodist Hymnal*)	"A Prayer of Saint Patrick" (No. 529 in *The United Methodist Book of Worship*) "The Apostolic Blessing" (No. 669 in *The United Methodist Hymnal*) "For Illumination" (No. 477 in *The United Methodist Hymnal*) "Psalm 133" (No. 850 in *The United Methodist Hymnal*)
Session Thirteen: We Worship God!	God's grace leads us to worship God. We worship God.	Psalm 95:6-7 (A call to worship)	"Go, Make of All Disciples" (No. 571 in *The United Methodist Hymnal*) "We Are the Church" (No. 558 in *The United Methodist Hymnal*) "Pass It On" (No. 572 in *The United Methodist Hymnal*)	"Litany for Christian Unity" (No. 556 in *The United Methodist Hymnal*) "For Guidance" (No. 366 in *The United Methodist Hymnal*) "Psalm 85" (No. 806 in *The United Methodist Hymnal*)

Section 2

Bulletin Inserts

A Service of Blessing for Those Entering the Study of Worship

Leader: As a community of believers, we come together to worship God. In our worship, we seek to see more clearly what God would want us to do as we live day by day. In our worship, we seek to feel God's presence in our lives. In our worship, we gain strength for sharing God's love with others. It is good when Christians come together for the purpose of learning more about why and how we worship. Our church is about to begin a study of worship. Will those who will be participating in this study, both leaders and students, come forward?

(Let all who will be participating come forward and kneel or stand at the altar rail.)

Pastor: Gracious God, we ask you to bless each one gathered here so that they may participate fully in this study and be enriched to more fully understand and participate in times of worship. Guide all who will be leading the sessions so that they may also grow in understanding as they prepare and as they lead. Give us the wisdom to use the gifts gained by all those who will be learning together so that they may contribute to our understanding and service. Amen.

Leader: Will you support these persons that are before you as they begin this time of study together?

Congregation: We affirm each person beginning this study. We promise to learn along with them, seeking always to grow in ways of relating to God and to others.

Pastor: May this be a time of learning, a time of blessing, and a time of growing for each of you. And may you feel the support of this congregation through-out the study.

(Those in the study may return to their seats at this time.)

A Service of Celebration Following Children Worship!

Study Leaders: It is with joy that we report to you that we have completed our study of worship. At this time we would like for those who participated in the study to come forward.

(Let all participants come forward and kneel or stand at the altar rail.)

Study Leaders: Those gathered before you have spent time in study together. They have engaged in activities to help them better understand why we gather to worship God and what we do when we gather to worship God. Not only have they been learners but they have been teachers to one another, helping all of us grow in our knowledge of God. This marks the end of the time of study. We ask you to rejoice with us at the completion of this study.

Congregation: We celebrate with you the completion of this study. We, too, are joyful for what you have learned and look forward to learning more from you as we worship together as a Christian community.

Pastor: Dear God, we thank you for this task that has been completed. We rejoice with these persons and give thanks for all that they have learned. Thank you for the gifts of these persons and the ways they have grown through this study. Guide us in using their gifts to your service in the church and in the world. We give thanks for those who have taught, thanking you for their steadfast leadership. Renew their strength for continued leadership for us all. Amen.

(If a gift, such as an altar cloth, has been prepared for the congregation, let members of the class present this gift on behalf of all the participants.)

Participants: We give thanks for this time of study and of learning. We trust God's blessings and know that we will continue to grow and to learn. We thank you for the support of this congregation. Thanks be to God!

All: Thanks be to God!

(Those in the study may return to their seats at this time.)

Preparing Our Children to Worship

Today, the children of our congregation begin a study about worship. During the next few weeks, they will learn about why we do what we do in worship services. They will talk about and participate in experiences that help them look at what we call the "movements" of worship: gathering, praising, praying, proclaiming God's Word, responding, and sending. As they learn, they will prepare for their own participation in worship as members of the family of God.

Worship, in many ways, is like a family meal. Individuals in a family can, and sometimes do, eat separately. However, there is deep enjoyment in sharing a meal with loved ones. Likewise, we sometimes worship independently and spontaneously, enjoying moments of beauty, peace, and joy as they occur. But if we never worshiped together as a church family, then we would miss an important element—the love present among the members of God's family.

As the children learn about worship, you will also have the opportunity to learn and to teach. Look for each of the upcoming bulletin inserts that describe what the children are studying. You can help the children grow in faith by utilizing the suggestions you will find in the inserts.

This week, pray for the children who are participating in this study. Pray that they will gain the knowledge that will enable them to become full participants in worship.

Smile at the children you see at church today. Express the joy you experience in worship through your facial expressions and body language. Children notice these things.

Call the children by name. Names are important to children, and when they are called by their names, they realize that you consider them important.

Listen to what the children have to say. Ask them what they are learning about worship and what they enjoy about your church.

Our Place of Worship

There are places where we gather to center our thoughts on God. Some of these are personal places, such as a quiet place in our home or a special place in nature. For most Christians the sanctuary of the church is one of the primary places where we gather to experience God.

Throughout Judeo-Christian history, people have built large gathering places to allow the whole community of faith to worship together. In the Bible we find the command to Moses to assemble the people—men, women, and children—that they might hear the Lord God (Deuteronomy 31:12). We gather to gain strength from one another, to focus our attention on God, and to encourage one another in following God's commandments.

Look around your church and your sanctuary. What do you see? What do you notice around you that helps you focus on God and on God's call in your life? Who are the people sitting near you? How many do you know? Who are the ones you call on for strength and help? Who among them have helped you know God in deeper ways?

Notice the items in the sanctuary. Notice the pictures, the symbols, the books. Locate the offering plates, the candles, the Bible stand, the banners. All of these are tools for worship. They help us focus on God. Which of these symbols have the most meaning for you?

Today, take the time to talk with one of the children about your sanctuary. Point out the things in the sanctuary that help you grow closer to God. Ask the child to tell you about what he or she likes best in the sanctuary.

Pray for the children as they continue their study.

Offering Praise and Thanks

Times of praise and thanks are found throughout the worship service. Sometimes we are unaware of how often we offer up words, songs, and gifts of praise and thanks during a worship service.

Think about who and what guides you through the worship service. The leaders who guide us do not worship for us; rather, they help us prepare to meet and know God's presence. Often when we gather for worship, we also have printed guides that help us know when to stand, when to sit, when to listen, and when to talk. These worship bulletins are also our guide.

Churches use different orders of worship; however, most contain the same parts. Here are some of the most common elements of worship:

- Prelude—Music helps us prepare to worship God.
- Introit—We are called, by music and/or word to worship God.
- First Hymn—We praise God with instruments and song.
- Responsive Reading—Together, we read God's Word from the Bible.
- Affirmation of Faith—We say what we believe.
- *Gloria Patri*—We sing praise to God.
- Prayers of Petition and Intercession—We pray to God for ourselves, for others, for our world.
- The Lord's Prayer—We pray together the prayer Jesus taught us.
- Concerns of the People—We hear how we care for those in our congregation and in our community.
- Offering—With thanks, we give gifts to God.
- Doxology—We praise God.
- Anthem—As the choir sings, we are reminded of God's goodness and care.
- Scripture—We hear God's Word from the Bible.
- Sermon—God's Word is explained and related to our lives.
- Hymn of Dedication—We promise to do God's work.
- Benediction—We go out to care for others and act as God would have us act.
- Postlude—Music sends us out to serve God.

Where do you see words, actions, and songs of praise and thanks in the order of worship?

Praising God Through Music

As children of God, we are called to a life of praise and thanksgiving for God's good gifts to us. One of the ways we most frequently offer our praise is through music. Early records show that music has been a fundamental part of our worship to God throughout history. It is a natural worship response.

Through music we are able to praise God with beautiful, lyrical words and expressive, moving melodies. The book of music we use most often in worship is our church's hymnal.

Think for a minute about books and how we are taught to read them. Now consider our hymnal. Most hymnals are put together in a manner that is very different from the books we read. Therefore, adults new to the faith and children just beginning to count and to read can be challenged by the hymnal format.

Children realize that the hymnal is an important book to have during worship because everyone has one. So, even before they can read or follow the stanzas, children are often seen holding the hymnal with pride. They realize that using this book is a part of being a member of the church family, and they want to feel that connection.

When you sit near a child, guide him or her in locating the appropriate hymns. Place bookmarks in the hymnal prior to the service so that there is less confusion as a new song begins. Help the child follow the lines of the hymns.

Let the children lead you in your appreciation of our hymns. Where the words are joyous, let your facial expression show the joy. Children will catch the spirit. Let the hymns truly reflect your praise and thanks to God.

We Gather to Pray

Prayer is an important part of every worship service. But prayer is not always something we feel comfortable doing. We are taught that this is our time to talk with God, but do we pray with the assurance that God is present with us? We are taught that prayer is the time to listen for God's direction in our lives, but do we pause long enough to hear God's voice? Often when we gather with other Christians to worship, we hurry through the prayers. We mumble the written responses, or do not say them at all.

Remember—children are watching. They form their opinions of prayer based partially on the way they see adults pray. Embrace the times of prayer during the worship service. Say the words of the printed prayers with conviction. Use the times of silence to open yourself to God. Attentively listen for those who are hurting and need God's comfort so that you can continue to pray for them throughout the week.

Remember, too, that children (and adults) learn from repetition. As we repeat familiar responses, we help our children possess the language for prayer.

In Matthew 6:9-13 we find a model prayer that Jesus gave to his disciples. It is so familiar to most of us that we usually say it without even thinking about the words. As you say the prayer today, consider the meaning of the words and say it with expression in your voice.

The Lord's Prayer can be used as a guide for all prayers: seeking God's will for our lives; asking and giving forgiveness; expressing praise and thankfulness.

We Pray in Many Ways

When the people of God come together for worship, they spend time talking with and listening to God. The time spent in prayer during worship is actually more than our regular recitation of the Lord's Prayer or our pause to listen to the pastor offer a prayer for the congregation. Look at the order of worship for today's service. Are there times when the people of God are to praise and to thank God? These are voiced or sung prayers. Are there times for the people of God to confess and ask God for forgiveness? Are there times for the people of God to petition God for needs they have? Are there times for the people of God to pray for others? These are times of prayer.

For children to grow in their ability to participate in worship, they need to recognize the language of prayer. Words used in and about prayer, such as *gloria*, *amen*, confession, forgiveness, and intercession are important for children to know. If you are sitting with a child and see one of these words, whisper an explanation so that the child will know what is being said in the prayer. Learning the language of prayer helps children feel more comfortable in using and hearing the words. This, in turn, provides a feeling of belonging.

When we gather for worship, we practice postures of prayer. We use these postures to show our relationship with God. Some bow their head to show honor and reverence. Some lift their head and hands to show their awe and wonder. Some kneel to show their obedience. Some pray with their eyes closed to focus solely on God. Some pray with their eyes open to notice God's wonderful world and the people who need God's love and care. See how many postures of prayer you use during the worship service.

The Book of God's People

The Bible is the book of God's people. As we read the Bible we see God active in history, speaking to others and calling them to service. The Bible tells us about Jesus and his example of how we should live. It calls us to faithfulness and challenges us to live as God would have us live. It provides inspiration and offers comfort. When we come together to worship, we are reminded of these lessons through God's Word.

Look at your bulletin. Where do you see the Bible used in the order of worship? Congregations usually have one to three Scripture readings each Sunday. Be a Bible explorer and you will usually discover others. Our responsive readings come from the Psalms, so we are reading Scripture as we respond. Many of the words of our hymns come from the Bible, so we are hearing Scripture as we sing.

Do you recall the story of Samuel? (Read 1 Samuel 3:1-10 if you have forgotten.) Samuel literally heard God call him in the night. Perhaps our calls from God are not quite as dramatic. Often, our calls come through the reading and the study of Scripture as we gather to worship, as we study with others, or as we study by ourselves. In the hearing and the reading of God's Word contained in the Bible, we open ourselves to God's touching our lives just as God touched the people of the Bible.

During the reading of the Scripture this week, make use of the pew Bible if your church provides one. If you bring your own Bible to use during the service, follow along as the Scripture is read. Help the children sitting near you find the book, chapter, and verses of the reading. Make notes about what you think God's Word is saying to you through today's Scripture. After the service ask some of the children what they heard and remembered from the Bible. Listen as they tell you their version of what was read. Encourage them to tell you what feelings they had about the Scripture. Talk with them about your feelings and thoughts.

Proclaiming the Word

When God's people gather for worship, they not only hear the Word of God read or sung from the Bible but also hear an interpretation. The purpose of the sermon is to help us understand the Scripture as it was written and its meaning for those at the time it was written. Another purpose of the sermon is to lead us in seeing God's call to us today as individuals and as a Christian community. The sermon helps us answer the questions, "Who do we need to be as a people of God?" and "What do we need to be doing as a people of God?" In the sermon, the preacher speaks for God (by the authority of the church) from the Scriptures to the people.

Many congregations have two sermons at each service: the children's sermon and what many call the "regular" sermon. The purpose of both is the same: to help us better hear and understand God's Word to us through the Scripture. Whenever the Word is proclaimed, take notes or write comments about what you hear. Raise questions when your interpretation seems to be different from that of the speaker's. Encourage the children who sit near you to listen for words they might not understand and to make notes or draw pictures as they listen to the sermon.

We also hear God's call through the Scripture in the statements of beliefs, or creeds, that we use in our churches. The most often used creed is the Apostles' Creed, which is more than twelve-hundred years old. Take time to read it as if you were seeing the creed for the first time. Think about the words. Remember that the word "catholic" means universal. The Apostles' Creed is the most universally used statement of our Christian faith, and it reflects our understanding of what we believe, based on what we learn from the Bible.

Celebrating the Seasons of the Church Year

What a changing world we live in! As God's creation changes, we move through the seasons of the year. As we celebrate the major events of our Christian faith, we move through the seasons of the church year. We celebrate days and seasons in the church because they remind us of the major events or themes of our Christian faith. When we gather to worship, our sanctuaries reflect each season of the church year as it is decorated with colorful paraments and banners. Not only do we proclaim the good news through the spoken word but also through the visual display of colors and symbols of the church year.

The chart shows the seasons, the colors we use to celebrate them, the major symbols, and reminders of what happens during each season.

The visual reminders of the seasons of the church year are important to all Christians, but they are particularly important to children. Take time to admire the colors and symbols you see around you in worship with a child. See what the child can tell you about the season and about the colors, and tell the child what you know about the seasons of the church year.

Bulletin Insert 9. © 1997 Discipleship Resources. Permission is given to reproduce this for use with Children Worship!

Season	Time	Colors	Symbol	What We Remember and Proclaim
Advent	Begins four Sundays before Christmas and continues until Christmas	Purple or Blue	Advent Wreath	Preparing for the coming of Christ
Christmas Season	Begins with Christmas Eve or Day and continues through the day of Epiphany (Jan. 6)	White and Gold	Manger	We praise and thank God for sending Jesus. On the day of Epiphany we remember the magi who came to see Jesus.
Season After the Epiphany (Ordinary Time)	Begins the day after the Epiphany and ends the day before Ash Wednesday	Green	Baptismal Font	Remembering the baptism of Jesus and the early ministry of Jesus
Lent	The forty days, not counting Sundays, that begin on Ash Wednesday and end on Holy Saturday	Purple; no color or black for Good Friday	Cross	Remembering the last days of Jesus' life
Easter Season (Great Fifty Days)	The fifty days beginning at sunset of Easter Eve and continuing through the Day of Pentecost	White and gold; red for the Day of Pentecost	Butterfly	We celebrate the resurrection of Christ. On the Day of Pentecost we celebrate the gift of the Holy Spirit.
Season After Pentecost (Ordinary Time)	Begins the day after Pentecost and ends the day before the first Sunday of Advent	Green	Triangle	Proclaiming the teachings of Jesus about the Kingdom of God

God's People Respond

Having heard God's Word through the Scriptures, the sermon, and the congregational responses during a worship service, God's people are to respond to what they have heard. There are many ways that we respond to God's call. In our worship services we respond in prayer and in statements of faith. We also respond through song, through giving, and through the sacraments of baptism and Holy Communion.

The word sacrament means "sacred moment." A sacrament is a special moment—a holy moment—when people come in contact with God. There are many times when this happens to us, and it can happen anywhere and at any time. The sacred moments that are scattered through our days and years allow us to continue responding to God's love and God's call of service to others. In our church we celebrate two particular sacred moments, baptism and Holy Communion. Jesus participated in these sacraments during his life on earth, and we are encouraged to do so as well.

We believe that baptism is an act of God through which we are initiated into the Christian community. Baptism is a sign and a means of God's grace. In baptism we are claimed as children of God. Because we are all completely dependent upon God, people of any age may be candidates for baptism.

Whatever the form of baptism—by sprinkling, pouring, or immersion—the symbol of water remains the same. Water is essential to life. It is cleansing and renewing.

When any person comes for baptism, the congregation promises to hold that person in Christian community. The congregation vows to surround the person in love and guide the person to grow in faith. It is the responsibility of each member of the congregation to fulfill the vows that are taken every time someone is baptized. Do not say them lightly. They carry a lifelong responsibility to be responsive to one another and assure that we continually grow together as disciples of Jesus Christ.

Talk with the children you see in worship. Ask about their activities and concerns. Ask what they are learning about God, about Jesus, and about the church. Share your faith experiences with them. Jesus loves us all. We are all a part of the family of God.

A Family Meal

Jesus ate many meals with his disciples, and they offered thanksgiving to God at those times. Jesus considered those who followed him as his family. At the Passover meal before his death and resurrection, Jesus gave his family (which includes us) a way to remember him and to continue to experience his presence.

In our church, we call this sacrament, Holy Communion, the Eucharist, or the Lord's Supper. As we partake, we remember Jesus and all that he taught us about God. We recognize the fellowship we have with one another. We respond to God's Word through Jesus and commit to lives of witness and service. This is a time rich in memory and in meaning.

Because of the depth of meaning in the service of Holy Communion, children do not understand every part of the service. Even as adults, can we fully comprehend the great sacrificial love that is remembered and experienced in Holy Communion? It is important to remember that children learn by doing first, then reflecting later as they grow. This is the kind of learning that takes place when our children participate in Holy Communion. When they come to the table, they are able to recognize that they are a part of God's family.

Talk with the children seated around you about the special meals they have in their families. Tell them about the meals that have great meaning for you, including Holy Communion.

Sent into the World

As a people of God gathered together for worship, we respond to God's love, ask for God's guidance, and look to God for strength and help as we pray. We hear God's Word through the Scripture, through readings, and through the sermon. We respond to God's Word, and we are sent into the world to love and serve God and our neighbors.

Sometimes when we reach the sending part of worship, we are too busy getting ready to leave to pay attention to what we are doing and saying. We mentally say, "Church is over. Time to get moving so we can make it to the restaurant before it gets too crowded." We are likely to miss the final action of worship: God sending us into the world.

Read Matthew 28:18-20. Jesus' words are not just for his disciples in the Bible; they are for us today. Reflect on how you use your gifts, your talents, your money, and your presence to witness to God's love and to serve your neighbor in the world.

It is through the community of believers that our witness to the world can be strengthened. As individuals, we certainly need to live a life that reflects all that God calls us to be. But when linked with other believers, our gifts extend to touch many more than we could imagine. Think about the gifts God gives us—time, abilities, education, human relationships, the environment, attitudes, our faith. These gifts are ours to use wisely. We do not simply leave a worship service. We are sent into the world to witness to God's love and to use these gifts in ways that reflect our belief in God's care and our certainty that we are to serve our neighbors through the use of those gifts.

If you are sitting near a child, call his or her attention to the actions of the acolytes at the end of the service. They do not extinguish the lights until the candlelighters are lit. They leave before anyone else, carrying the light of God's love into the world. We follow that light. We increase that light by our actions so that all the world may know the God revealed by Jesus Christ.

All God's Children

Today as you sit in worship, look around you. What are the ages of those gathered together today to worship God? Do you see people across the life span? Young and old, we are called by God to worship God. Young and old, we are called to gather with the community of believers in Jesus Christ, to listen to God, and to seek to serve God. Young and old, we offer our gifts to God and seek to leave our places of worship renewed in our faith and strengthened to serve the world.

Look at the young around you. Jesus gave us two portraits of children among his followers in the New Testament. Do you remember the story of Jesus and the children? You may want to read this story, which is found in Luke 18:15-17, again. When the disciples scolded people for bringing their children to Jesus, Jesus said, "Let the little children come to me, and do not stop them; for it is to such as these that the kingdom of God belongs." Children belong in the community of faith.

Remember, too, the boy who shared his food. Turn to John 6:1-13, and read again what happened when those gathered to hear Jesus were hungry. When the crowd grew hungry and the disciples wondered what to do, Andrew said, "There is a boy here who has five barley loaves and two fish." The boy served the community of faith by sharing his food. And through the power of Jesus, all were fed. Children can play a responsible part in the life of the community of faith.

How is it in your congregation today? How are the children included? How do children lead and play responsible roles when the people gather to worship God?

As you worship, and after the service, you can help children feel that they truly belong and truly serve by:

- speaking to children, calling them by name.
- asking a child to pray with you about a concern you share as Christians in the same faith community.
- pointing out the things in your sanctuary that help you focus on God and asking a child to show you the things that help him or her focus on God.
- sharing a hymnal or a Bible and helping each other read or sing the words.
- thanking children for the contributions they have made in today's worship—as Bible readers, as acolytes, as greeters, as choir members, or in any other way in which they provide leadership.

Section 3

Letters to the Parents

Dear Parent,

Your child is invited to participate in a study about how we worship as a community of believers in Jesus Christ.

We believe that coming together to worship God is essential for growing Christians. In a community of worshipers, we can learn more about God and God's plans, and we can support one another in living in a way that reflects God's love and care.

The study *Children Worship!* has been designed to help children strengthen their participation in congregational worship. As children understand what we do in worship, they can participate more fully. During the weeks of this study, we will examine the different parts of worship. We will learn about the sacraments of baptism and Communion. We will practice participating in the different parts of the worship service.

During these sessions, your child will be involved in active learning. We will use many activities to help your child understand and enjoy learning about worship. Each week your child will bring home a letter outlining what we have done in the day's session and what you may want to do at home to reinforce the learnings. We hope these suggestions will enrich your home worship and will provide a way of talking together about God and about how we seek to know and serve God.

Our study will begin on _____ and will continue through _____. We feel that each child needs to be present at as many sessions as possible to obtain the fullest benefit from this study.

It is our hope that you will choose for your child to participate in this study. You can help us plan more effectively by letting us know by _____ if your child plans to attend. We will send further information about our study two weeks before we begin.

If you have questions, please contact _____ at _____.

Dear Parent,

You and your child are invited to participate in a study about the ways we worship as a community of believers in Jesus Christ.

We believe that coming together to worship God is essential for growing Christians. In a community of worshipers, we can learn more about God and God's plans, and we can support one another in living in a way that reflects God's love and care.

The study *Children Worship!* has been designed to help children and their families strengthen their participation in congregational worship. As we understand what we do in worship, we can participate more fully. During the weeks of this study, we will examine the different parts of worship. We will learn about the sacraments of baptism and Communion. We will practice participating in the different parts of the worship service.

During these sessions, you and your child will be involved in active learning. We will use many activities to help everyone understand and enjoy learning about worship. Each week we will send home with you a letter outlining what we have done in the day's session and what you may want to do at home to reinforce the learnings. We hope these suggestions will enrich your home worship and will provide a way of talking together about God and about how we seek to know and serve God.

Our study will begin on _____ and will continue through _____. We feel that all participants need to be present at as many sessions as possible to obtain the fullest benefit from this study.

It is our hope that you will choose to participate with your child in this study. You can help us plan more effectively by letting us know by _____ if you plan to attend. We will send further information about our study two weeks before we begin.

If you have questions, please contact _____ at _____.

Dear Parent,

We are looking forward to your child's participation in *Children Worship!*

Our first session is scheduled for _____ at _____. Please bring your child to
_____. The following adult leaders will be there to greet you and your child:
_____.

In preparation for this first session, we ask that you begin talking with your child about worship. You may want to help your child think about the things you enjoy in worship. You may want to talk about why worship is important to you. Notice the things in your home that help you worship. We ask that you pray for the leaders and the children who will be participating in these sessions.

During the worship service on Sunday, _____, the congregation will be asked to affirm the work of the children in these sessions. We will ask that all families who are involved in the study to stand to receive the prayers and affirmations of the congregation.

Please assist us by helping your child look forward to this time of learning. We consider it a joy and a privilege to work with your child. If you have questions, call _____ at
_____. We will see you and your child on _____.

Dear Parent,

We look forward to having you and your child participate in *Children Worship!*

Our first session is scheduled for _____ at _____. Please come to
_____. The following leaders will be there to greet you and your child:
_____.

In preparation for this first session, we ask that you begin talking with your child about worship. You may want to help your child think about the things you enjoy in worship. You may want to talk about why worship is important to you. Notice things in your home that help you worship. We ask that you pray for all who will be participating in these sessions.

During the worship service on Sunday, _____, the congregation will be asked to affirm the work of your family in these sessions. We will ask that all families involved in the study to stand to receive the prayers and affirmations of the congregation.

Please assist us by helping your child look forward to this time of learning. We consider it a joy and a privilege to work with your family. If you have questions, call _____ at _____. We will see you and your child on _____.

Dear Parent,

Today marked the beginning of our worship study with your child. We are excited about what we have done today. We hope that you will be able to continue that excitement through some activities at home during the week.

In the Bible we read of the time when Jesus participated in leading worship. As followers of Jesus, we too are called to worship. We seek to know God and to realize God's will for living in community with others.

We have talked today about the first movement of worship: gathering. When we come together to worship, we find strength as a people of God, and we feel God's presence.

We want to encourage you to talk with your child about the worship study, about the worship service itself, and about the people in our church family.

DURING THE WEEK

1. Help your child talk about times when he or she feels close to God. Mention the times during the day when you feel close to God.

2. Read one or more of the following Scriptures with your child:
   - Luke 4:16-21 (where Jesus led in worship)
   - Psalm 98:4-6 (showing a joyous, celebrative time of worship)
   - Psalm 46:10 (showing a quiet, personal time of worship)
   - 1 John 4:19 (which reminds us that we love because God first loved us)

3. Pray together each night. Pray for specific people in your congregation and for those who lead your worship services.

We look forward to seeing your child in our second session.

Dear Parent,

Today, our study centered on the sanctuary and on the tools of worship found there. The word sanctuary means "a safe place" or a "holy place." We talked about and saw pictures of church sanctuaries and the other places people go to feel close to God—peaceful spots in nature and quiet areas in the home.

We also talked about some of the tools of worship found in the sanctuary. These tools include the Bible, the cross, the candles, the hymnal, the offering plates, the bulletin, the paraments, the water used for baptism, the Communion elements, and the candlelighters.

Many sanctuaries have sacred art or stained glass windows. These are in our sanctuaries because their beauty helps us focus on God. Your child made a stained glass window today. Perhaps you and your child can find a place to hang this in your home as a reminder of God.

Your child has begun a worship folder. Each week your child will write or draw in this folder. When the study ends, your child will have a week-by-week memory book of what he or she learned.

DURING THE WEEK

1. Talk with your child about the places that are important to you in your spiritual life. It can be a place in the house where you privately study the Bible or pray. It can be a place outdoors or a particular location that you visit occasionally. Help your child find a place in your home for private prayer and thought about God.

2. This week, take your child to the sanctuary in your church or a sanctuary of a church near you. Sit quietly, enjoying the stillness, and listen to God.

3. Read Psalm 95:1-7a, Psalm 122:1, and Luke 2:41-52 with your child. Talk about what happens in each of these examples of worship.

4. Look around your house for tools of worship. Check each room to see if there are symbols, pictures, or items that help you focus on God.

Dear Parent,

Today, we began our study of how we praise and thank God when we come together for worship. To help us do this, we explored the worship bulletin and looked for the times and ways we give thanks and praise.

We talked in particular about the Doxology. (A doxology is any hymn or prayer of praise to the Trinity.) You may want to sing this with your child and discuss how the words praise God for everything on the earth.

We also offer praise and thanks to God at the time of offering. Remember that offerings include our money, our talents, our time, and our service. We give all of these as a way to praise and thank God for God's gifts to us.

DURING THE WEEK

1. Read Psalm 111:1, a psalm of thanks and praise. Say this several times together during the week.

2. Help your child identify times when he or she praises or thanks God. Mention the times during the day when you say thanks or praise.

3. Have a morning and evening time of praise and thanks with your child at some point during the week.

4. Look at the Sunday worship bulletin. Review with your child the order of worship and look for times of praise and thanks.

Dear Parent,

Today, we finished our study of how we praise and thank God when we come together for worship. During our time together, we learned about the hymnal and used it to find hymns we enjoy. We began learning the *Gloria Patri* as a song that helps us praise God. We talked about how the words are in the Latin language, and they mean "Glory to the Father."

The hymns and songs of the church help us express our praise and thanks to God, and they put us in a worshipful mood. The songs of faith learned in childhood can increasingly become more meaningful as children mature.

The hymnal is an important book for your child to learn to use. As your child becomes familiar with the hymnal, he or she can participate more fully in the worship service. You can assist by examining and working with the hymnal at home. Borrow a hymnal from church or purchase one. Go through the hymnal, locating the hymns you enjoy. Talk to your child about these. Help your child locate hymns he or she remembers and enjoys.

DURING THE WEEK

1. Practice the *Gloria Patri* and the Doxology at home. Your child can learn the words by writing the phrases on individual strips of paper. Put these papers in order on a tabletop. After singing the response a few times with the words, turn over a strip and sing the response by filling in the missing words from memory. Continue to turn over strips and sing as long as your child wishes.

2. Sung responses are a way of praising God. Praise is saying something good about someone or to someone. Use the word praise often in your conversations so that it is a familiar term for your child.

3. Read Psalm 98:4-6, a song of praise. This helps us know it is good to praise God with song.

4. Choose a hymn for the week and learn it together. Sing it often as you are together, working or playing, riding in the car, or waiting in a line. Make this a hymn you enjoy together. Talk with your child about why this hymn has meaning for you.

Dear Parent,

Today, we have completed the first of two sessions on prayer. When God's people come together for worship, they pray, sharing their concerns with God, asking for guidance, and listening for God's Word for their lives. We have spent most of our time studying the Lord's Prayer.

Learning prayers can be compared to learning swimming strokes. Repetition and practice are essential. Learned prayers prepare us to talk to God in our own words.

When Jesus' disciples asked how they should pray, he gave them an example. We use this example of prayer in our churches today. In praying this prayer, we open ourselves to God. It is important for children to learn the Lord's Prayer, even when they cannot understand it all. As they say this prayer with the adults during Sunday worship, they feel included. This is meaningful for them in ways we cannot measure. As they grow, this prayer will continue to have meaning, growing and changing with them through the years.

DURING THE WEEK

1. Talk with your child about the words from the Lord's Prayer. Here is some information that may be helpful:
   - thy and thine—Old words for "your" and "yours."
   - your kingdom come, your will be done—We pray that everyone on earth will live according to the way God wants us to live.
   - our daily bread—God is dependable. God will take care of us.
   - sin, trespasses, debts—This is what separates us from God.
   - as we forgive—We realize we are to forgive others as God forgives us.
   - save us from the time of trial, but deliver us from evil—God's help is available to us.
   - Amen—This is a word of thanksgiving and praise that can be interpreted as a loud "yes."

2. Read Matthew 6:9-13. Focus on the words. Say the Lord's Prayer. Ask your child to name the differences between the prayer as we say it and the story about it in the Bible.

3. Talk with your child about when you learned the Lord's Prayer. Relate your learning the prayer to the experience your child is now having.

Dear Parent,

Today, we have completed the second session on prayer. When God's people come together for worship, they talk with God through prayer.

It is important for children to realize that we pray not only at church but also at home, at school, in the car, and on the playground. We pray as we rise in the morning, throughout the day, at mealtimes, and as we go to bed at night.

When we pray, we talk with God in different ways. We offer prayers of praise and thanks as we recall God's greatness and goodness and God's bountiful blessings in this world. We offer prayers of confession and forgiveness as we remember the things we have done and said that do not reflect the way God would want us to live, and we ask God to forgive us. We offer prayers of petition as we ask God for the things we feel that we need. We offer prayers of intercession as we ask God to be with others.

When they are young, children more clearly understand the prayers of thanks and praise. As they grow, they begin to understand other types of prayer. Guide them in all of the ways they can talk with God.

DURING THE WEEK

1. Read Psalm 9:1-2 and 1 Thessalonians 5:16-18 with your child.

2. Find with your child a place in your home that can be your prayer corner. Decide what needs to go in the corner to help you think about God. Include pictures that help you focus on God, items from the natural world, and a Bible. Use this corner as a place for individual prayer.

3. Pick a different prayer for morning, evening, and meals. This could be a verse from the Bible, a printed prayer from church materials, or a prayer you write together. Learn this prayer and say it for one week.

4. At the end of each day, talk with your child about the joys and concerns of the day. Be intentional about naming the things that have made you happy for yourself or for others. Remember the concerns of your family, the concerns of the people you know, and the concerns for the world that you hear about or see on television.

Dear Parent,

Today, we started the first of two sessions on proclaiming God's Word. This week we focused on the Bible. Scripture has always been a part of our Christian worship. Through the Scriptures, we hear God's Word proclaimed and can reflect on what God's call is for us today.

Although we know how important the Bible is to our faith, it may still seem difficult to find the time to read and study the Scripture. What do you do now that helps you have the time for personal Bible study? What can you begin doing to help your child develop Bible study habits?

Our children first learn about the Bible by seeing adults they love reading it. This example helps them realize that the Bible is an important book. Our children also learn when we read to them from our Bible, from a children's Bible, or Bible storybooks. This helps them know that the Bible stories are also for them. Our children continue to learn when we ask questions—"What do you think this story (or this verse) means for us today?" "How are we like Abraham (or Sarah, or Ruth, or Peter)?" These discussions help our children reflect on the message of the Bible.

DURING THE WEEK
1. Read these stories from the Bible with your child:
   • 1 Samuel 3:1-10 (God calls to Samuel, and Samuel listened to God.)
   • Psalm 23 (God will care for us.)
   • Luke 18:15-17 (Jesus includes children.)

2. Look for Bibles in your home. See how many you have and where they are located. Talk with your child about the Bibles you have, sharing memories of when you received them and what they mean to you.

3. Tell each other Bible stories or recite verses from the Bible daily. Mention the ones that have meaning for you. Let your child tell you about the ones he or she enjoys.

4. When you read with your child at bedtime, include Bible storybooks with the other books you read together.

Dear Parent,

Today, we continued our study of the ways God's Word is proclaimed in our worship service. We talked about sermons, and we talked about creeds, or statements of belief.

The sermon serves as an interpretation of Scripture. We believe that the sermon helps us discover the connection between the Scriptures and our daily living. Since the sermon is often the longest uninterrupted time of listening during the worship service, children often have trouble sitting still and following what is being said. Remember the following: First, adults too have difficulty listening to and focusing on the sermon, particularly if it is over twelve minutes in length. Second, children can listen and do other things at the same time. They can draw and still pay attention to what is being said. In fact, sometimes this helps them pay closer attention. Keep pens and paper with you in worship so that your child may draw or write when the "listening time" gets long.

We included creeds, or statements of belief, with proclaiming because these statements reflect our understanding of Scripture and its call to faith. The Apostles' Creed is more than 1,200 years old, and it is one of the oldest statements of belief we have. Many statements are found in the hymnal. You may want to look through several of these statements and determine which ones most closely reflect your faith.

DURING THE WEEK

1. Read Peter's sermon found in Acts 3:11-26 with your child. Recall other sermons you have heard recently. Act out some of the things described or suggested in those sermons.

2. Read a story told by Jesus. Discuss with your child what you would say if you were going to preach a sermon using that Scripture.

3. Talk about the ideas that were presented in the Scripture and the sermon during last Sunday's worship service. Discuss what you heard, and how you have thought about the sermon during week. Your child will begin to realize that the sermon can make us think and reflect on what we believe and how we act on days other than Sunday.

4. Practice saying the Apostles' Creed with your child. Talk together about the words contained in the creed, explaining what you think they mean and what you believe.

Dear Parent,

Today, we learned about the special days and seasons of the church year. In our worship services, we observe a rhythm of time that reflects Jesus' birth, life, death, and resurrection, as well as the coming of the Holy Spirit.

The way that we spend our time indicates what we consider important. We come together for worship on Sundays as a weekly remembrance of Jesus' resurrection and as a celebration of life with God. Like most of the things that happen in worship, this rhythm of celebration needs to carry into our home life as well. We live in witness to our faith through the year.

This chart shows the seasons, the colors we use to celebrate them, major symbols of the season, and reminders of what happens during the seasons.

DURING THE WEEK

1. Read these Bible passages:
   - Luke 1:39-56 (Advent)
   - Matthew 27:27-50 (Lent)
   - Luke 2:1-20 (Christmas Season)
   - Matthew 28 (Easter Season)
   - Matthew 2:1-12 (Epiphany)
   - Acts 2:1-4 (Pentecost)
   - Matthew 3:13-17 (Season After the Epiphany)
   - Matthew 18:1-5 (Season After Pentecost)

2. Make symbols for the seasons. Use the traditional symbols or let your child decide which symbols would be best for a given season. Listen to his or her explanations.

3. Decide on a place that could be your worship center at home. Place items in this space that remind you of the current season.

4. Talk about family traditions that help you celebrate the church year. Decide on new traditions you would like to begin.

Season	Time	Colors	Symbol	What We Remember and Proclaim
Advent	Begins four Sundays before Christmas and continues until Christmas	Purple or Blue	Advent Wreath	Preparing for the coming of Christ
Christmas Season	Begins with Christmas Eve or Day and continues through the day of Epiphany (Jan. 6)	White and Gold	Manger	We praise and thank God for sending Jesus. On the day of Epiphany we remember the magi who came to see Jesus.
Season After the Epiphany (Ordinary Time)	Begins the day after the Epiphany and ends the day before Ash Wednesday	Green	Baptismal Font	Remembering the baptism of Jesus and the early ministry of Jesus
Lent	The fourty days, not counting Sundays, that begin on Ash Wednesday and end on Holy Saturday	Purple; no color or black for Good Friday	Cross	Remembering the last days of Jesus' life
Easter Season (Great Fifty Days)	The fifty days beginning at sunset of Easter Eve and continuing through the Day of Pentecost	White and gold; red for the Day of Pentecost	Butterfly	We celebrate the resurrection of Christ. On the Day of Pentecost we celebrate the gift of the Holy Spirit.
Season After Pentecost (Ordinary Time)	Begins the day after Pentecost and ends the day before the first Sunday of Advent	Green	Triangle	Proclaiming the teachings of Jesus about the Kingdom of God

Dear Parent,

Today, we began our study of the fifth movement of worship: responding to God's Word. Having heard God's Word through the Scripture, the sermon, and the hymns, God's people have the opportunity to respond to what they have heard. There are many ways that we respond to God's call. In our worship services we respond in prayer and in statements of faith. We respond through song and through giving. We respond through the sacraments of baptism and Holy Communion.

The word sacrament means "sacred moment." A sacrament is a special moment—a holy moment—when people come in contact with God. There are many times when this happens to us, and it can happen anywhere and at any time. The sacred moments scattered through our days and years allow us to continue responding to God's love and God's call for service to others. In our church we celebrate two particular sacred moments, baptism and Holy Communion. These are sacraments that Jesus participated in during his life on earth, and we are encouraged to do so as well.

We studied baptism today. Through baptism we are claimed by God, and we respond in faith and love. The Holy Spirit is already at work in the lives of children brought to baptism and in the lives of adults seeking baptism on their own. Both respond by striving to live their lives in a way that increases their faith and service as disciples of Jesus Christ.

DURING THE WEEK

1. Read with your child about the story of Jesus' baptism (Mark 1:9-11) and the stories of the baptisms of others in the New Testament, including the baptism of the Ethiopian official (Acts 8:38-40) and the baptism of Lydia (Acts 16:11-15). Talk about how these compare with the baptisms you may have seen in your congregation. Explain to your child that although there are differences, these baptisms are the same as today's.

2. If your child was baptized as an infant, tell him or her about the event. If you saved mementos of that day, show these to your child. Find the date your child was baptized, and write it on your calendar. Make plans to celebrate this baptism day with your child.

3. Talk with your child about water and how it is used in baptism. Talk about the uses of water in our life: It gives us life, it cleanses, and it refreshes. Make a list of all the ways you use water in your home. Listen to your child tell you why we use water in baptism.

4. The next time someone is baptized in your congregation, let your child make a card for the person, welcoming them to the church family.

Dear Parent,

Today, we continued our study about the ways we respond to God in worship. We talked about how we are a family during Holy Communion (the Lord's Supper). During the sacrament we remember that Jesus proved how much God loves us.

In our churches this sacrament is referred to in different ways: Holy Communion, the Lord's Supper, the Eucharist. Children may become confused by the distinctions implied in the names. Simply explain to them that all of the terms are used for the same service, but the meaning of the service can be described in many ways.

The Lord's Supper is a time to remember. We remember the life of Jesus, especially the meal he shared with his friends in the upper room. Holy Communion is a time when we feel the power of God's grace and love. We recall the times when we did not act as God would want us to act, but we also remember that God loves and forgives us. We experience God's presence and remember the sacrifice that Jesus made for our sake. We see the bread and the juice as symbols of Jesus' blood and body. And we come together for a family meal, recognizing that we are a people of God and that we belong to God's family.

As children participate in Holy Communion they understand that they are an important part of God's family. As they continue to grow in their faith, they will grow in their understanding of the significance of the sacrament. The Lord's Supper is a family meal, and all members of the family are welcome.

DURING THE WEEK
1. Read the following biblical passages together:
   • Exodus 12:1-20 (the story of the Passover)
   • Matthew 26:26-29, Mark 14:22-25, and Luke 22:12-20 (accounts of the Last Supper)
   • 1 Corinthians 11:23-26 (the gathering of the early church to celebrate Communion)

2. Make an effort to have a family meal one time this week. Dress up and come to the table with the expectations of celebrating being part of the family. Talk about the times when you feel counted as an important member in your family and the times when you feel included as an important part of God's family at church.

3. Bake bread together, and eat it while it is still warm. Talk about the way we are nourished by bread and why this is an important symbol for Christians.

4. Bake cookies or bread with your child, and, together, take your gift of food to a neighbor or a church member who is lonely. Allow enough time to visit and pray with the person you visit.

Dear Parent,

Today, we have talked about the final action of worship: sending. When we leave the worship service, our action is not ending; it is only beginning. We are sent into the world to live as God would have us live, showing God's love to others and inviting them to join us as brothers and sisters in Christ.

The sending usually includes the benediction and dismissal, yet there are other examples of this empowerment in our worship. We are sent into the world through the blessings for and the services of commission for particular jobs on behalf of the church. The acolytes symbolize God's sending disciples into the world. At the end of the service, the acolytes carry the light out of the sanctuary and into the world. We follow, also carrying the light of Jesus with us. That light is reflected in our actions as we work and play, at home and in our community.

From early childhood, your child has been learning from your example. Through play, many young children act out what they see in the lives of the adults who are close to them. This is not only a way of learning but how the child seeks to be a part of the adult world. Through your example of service, your child is learning what it means to be a disciple of Jesus Christ.

DURING THE WEEK

1. Read Matthew 28:18-20 with your child. Discuss the ways you remind each other of Jesus and the ways you help each other know his teachings.

2. Help your child set aside a portion of his or her allowance to give to God through the church. If your church has offering envelopes, see that your child has some envelopes to use.

3. As a family, talk about the ways you can serve God individually or as a unit. Suggestions: regularly visiting an older adult in your neighborhood or congregation; recycling items at home that would have otherwise gone into the trash; helping prepare and serve meals at a homeless shelter; writing to a missionary; reading to children in a daycare center in your neighborhood; or helping clean the church yard.

4. Bless your child each day. Before your child goes to bed each night, lay your hands on his or her head. Thank God for your child, and ask God to bless your child.

Dear Parent,

Today was the final session of our study on worship. Thank you for the encouragement and support you have given to the teachers and to your child as they have participated in these sessions.

Although this ends our study on worship, we hope that what we have done in these sessions will continue to guide you and your child as you worship together in church and at home. Part of being a parent is being a constant model and teacher. Your child will continue to watch how you worship in church and at home. The lessons they learn from watching you will be much more lasting than those we have enjoyed over the past weeks.

We have learned much about worship and why we do what we do when we gather as a people of God. When your child enters worship, the things seen and heard will have more meaning. Remember, however, that even with these new learnings, children will still wiggle. Children will still ask questions at inappropriate times. Children will still become weary of sitting. Children will still need explanations about what is happening and why we do what we do.

As parents, we must continue to worship God as we help our children worship. Remember, parenting is a calling. We are called by God to nurture, to love, to teach, and to guide our children in ways that lead them closer to God. Even though they have completed these sessions, they have not arrived. They have only completed a portion of the journey of growing in faith.

Remember, too, that you are not alone. Every member of the congregation vowed with you to guide and uphold your child in faith through the covenant of baptism. Call upon these partners to be examples, friends, teachers, and partners with you and your child. As followers of Jesus Christ, we find strength and support in community.

Continue guiding your child for worship at church and at home by
- finding regular times to read from the Bible and to read Bible storybooks together.
- praying daily for your child and with your child.
- seeking ways you and your child can serve God and serve others in your community.
- celebrating the holy days and holidays of the church at home.
- singing hymns in your everyday life and in your home.

Section 4

Session Plans

Session One
We Gather to Worship

Main Idea

God's grace calls us together in community. God's people come together to praise and worship God.

Purpose

Participants will

• experience the joy of praising God.

• learn why coming together for worship is important for Christians.

Bible in This Session

1. Luke 4:16-21 (Jesus worshiped regularly.)
2. Psalm 98:4-6 (Corporate worship is a joyous, celebrative time.)
3. Psalm 46:10 (Worship is sometimes quiet and personal.)
4. 1 John 4:19 (We love God because God first loved us.)

Background for Teachers

Worship is sometimes defined as becoming aware of God's presence. For all who come together in the community of the church, God is central. Worship is recognizing the importance of God in our lives. In worship we celebrate God's love by listening to God's Word for us and by responding in faith.

As we are reminded in the passages from Psalm 98 and Psalm 46, worship can be both noisy, celebrative, and in the midst of people; it can also be quiet, reflective, and personal.

But, as we come together, the shared experience of worship can increase our receptivity to God and our awareness of God. Through our worshiping community we experience God and open ourselves to respond to God. We call those who gather the "congregation." Congregation means "to lock together;" therefore, the word itself reminds us that we worship God as a group.

As a leader, you can help participants recognize the many forms of our response to God. They can identify times in their lives when they have felt God, or talked with God, or thought about God. This might have been through bedtime or mealtime prayers. It could have been as they looked at a sunset. It could have been as they stood with their family and recited the Lord's Prayer with others in the congregation. Invite all of the participants to share when they have felt close to God. Listen to their stories of God in their lives. Talk about your own experiences of God through worship.

Preparing to Teach

1. Read the entire unit to see how Session One fits into the bigger plan for the study.
2. Read Session One.
3. Copy "Bulletin Insert 1" and collate it into the church's Sunday worship bulletin. If the sessions are being held on a day other than Sunday, use this bulletin on the Sunday following the first session. If you are using the

study as an intergenerational one, make appropriate modifications to the insert.

4. Find "This Is the Day" (No. 657) in *The United Methodist Hymnal*. If you are unfamiliar with the hymn, ask another adult to help you learn it.

5. Check the materials list and gather the supplies needed for the activities.

6. Copy "Hidden Message" (p. 59) for each participant.

7. Prepare a nametag for each person. See the pattern and instructions on page 60. Cut the nametags apart and mount each on a piece of construction paper or lightweight posterboard. Punch two holes in the top of the nametag and tie an end of a twenty-four-inch piece of yarn through each hole.

8. Copy the "Letter to Parents" for Session One for each child to take home after the session.

9. Duplicate a set of the "Beginnings' Cards" (p. 58). Cut the cards apart and mount each on a piece of construction paper or an index card.

10. Set up a worship center. Include an open Bible, a cross, and a candle.

Materials

1. Balloons (or paper cutouts) and permanent markers
2. Bible
3. Yarn
4. Pencils
5. Paper towel cardboard tubes
6. Wax paper
7. Rubber bands
8. Wide elastic
9. Jingle bells (at least four per person)
10. Small safety pins or a needle and thread
11. "Beginnings' Cards"
12. Nametags
13. 11- by 16-inch construction paper or pocket folders

THE SESSION PLAN

BEGINNING ACTIVITIES (5-10 minutes)
As the participants enter the room, invite them to write their names on a nametag and to color one of the church symbols on the nametag. They should then move to the area where you have placed the balloons and markers. Give each child a balloon or a balloon cutout. Ask them to draw or write on the balloon something they do when they are in worship (or "big church") with their family. Be ready with suggestions of things we do in church. When all are finished, have them gather in a circle.

GROUP TIME (15-20 minutes)
Ask the participants to describe what they have drawn or written. Then say, "Today is our first session together. We'll be meeting several more times, and each time we meet we're going to talk about worship. Let's see if we can discover what we mean when we say the word, 'worship.'"

Give each person a copy of "Hidden Message" and a marker. Tell the group they can discover the message by marking out all of the "Q's." If there are adults and children in your group, let each child work with an adult to find the message. When they are finished say, "In a few minutes you may take your activity sheet and decorate it, but right now we're going to talk together about the hidden message."

When you have read the message, discuss its meaning. Explain that we attend worship because we believe in God and want to be with others who believe in God. Define the congregation as the people who gather together in worship. Tell the class that they are going to learn about the things that help us hear and speak with God.

Say, "We'll be learning a lot about the time when we come together in worship. Today, we're only talking about the beginning part—the 'getting-there' part. I'm going to ask you to tell me some of the things you do to get ready for church. I'll name some too. When any of us names something you do to get ready for church and for worship, stand up. If someone says something you don't do, sit down."

Guide the group if it seems stuck by mentioning the items listed below. Make sure to mention other specific things that your congregation does as it gathers for worship. You may want to add some things that clearly are not done to create more movement and to make the activity more fun.

• Getting dressed
• Bringing a Bible
• Receiving a bulletin from an usher
• Watching the choir enter the choir loft
• Saying hello to others who are in worship
• Seeing the candles lit
• Seeing the worship leader motion for us to stand at the beginning of the service
• Hearing the pastor greet the congregation

Thank the group for participating. Say, "Now, we're going to look at a book in the Bible that tells us how people worship." After turning to beginning of the Book of Psalms, show the open Bible to the class. Explain that the Psalms give examples of the many different ways and times we can worship. The passages selected illustrate two ways. First, read Psalm 98:4-6. Ask the group to mention some things that people do when they are joyful. Think also of the times when joy is expressed during worship.

Now read Psalm 46:10. Ask the group to think of the quiet times during worship. Have a short time of silence. Then pray together asking God to be with you in your times of study.

ACTIVITIES (20-30 minutes)
Play a Game
Use the "Beginnings' Cards" (p. 58). Start the game by asking a participant to draw a card. That person then acts out what the person on the card is doing to signify that it is time to begin worship. With younger children, it helps to whisper suggestions. If you have an intergenerational group, you may want to pair an adult with a child or pair an older child with a younger child. The rest of the group is to guess who is being portrayed. When the person has been correctly identified, place the drawn card on the bottom of the stack. Invite another person to draw a card and act it out. Everyone should have a turn.

Make Instruments
Let each participant choose to make either a horn or a bell bracelet.

Bell Bracelets
Cut six-inch pieces of elastic and four-inch pieces of yarn. Give each person four bells. Show them how to slip the yarn through the bell loop and tie it to the elastic. Fasten the two ends of the elastic together with small safety pins, or stitch them together with a needle and thread.

Horns
Give each person a paper towel cardboard tube. Using felt-tipped markers, decorate the outside of the tube. (Caution them to use a gentle touch to avoid crushing the tube.) Put a piece of wax paper over one end of the tube, and secure it with a rubber band.

Complete the Activity Sheet
Provide markers or crayons and let the participants decorate their activity sheets with things that remind them of worship.

Make a Worship Folder

Give each person a pocket folder or a piece of 11- by 16-inch construction paper that has been folded in half. Print the word WORSHIP on the chalkboard. Have the participants write "Worship" and their names on the outside of their folder. Using felt-tipped markers, they should decorate their folders with words or pictures that remind them of how we worship God. When they have finished, have them place their activity sheets in their folders. Explain that they will complete something each week that will go into the folders. When they have completed the course, they will have a memory book that helps them to recall what they learned about worship.

WORSHIP (5 minutes)

Invite everyone to bring his or her class-made instrument to the worship table. While standing together around the table, sing "This Is the Day" (No. 657 in *The United Methodist Hymnal)*, and use the instruments to accompany the hymn. This is an easy-to-learn hymn, even for non-reading children, since the leader sings a line before the group repeats it.

Read 1 John 4:19. Together, pray to and thank God for this time of learning about worship.

Distribute the "Letters to the Parents" for Session One. If parents are participating in the sessions, explain that you will be giving them a weekly reminder of what happened during the sessions and some suggestions for reinforcing these learnings in their homes. Children whose parents do not attend should be reminded each week to give the letters to their parents.

IF YOU HAVE MORE TIME

1. If you are meeting at a time when the sanctuary is not in use, take the class to the sanctuary. Ask the group to notice as many things as they can. You may want to try the "ABC' method of observation. Beginning with the letter "A," ask the group to find an item in the sanctuary that begins with that letter. Continue the process through the rest of the alphabet.

2. Watch a videotape of your congregation at worship, or listen to an audiotape of your service. Your church may routinely videotape worship services. If not, you may be able to borrow a member's videotape of a baptism or another important service. Use an audiotape only if you do not have a videotape. Play only a portion of the tape—a segment lasting no more than seven minutes. Discuss what the group noticed about the people and the service.

3. Play the Going to Church Game. Sit in a circle. Begin by saying, "My name is (state your name). I'm going to church, and I'm going to take a (name something that begins with the first initial of your name) with me." Ask the person next to you to state his or her name and choice of item. Then, he or she needs to repeat your name and item. Have the next person complete the sentence and recall what was named by the people before. This continues until all have had a turn. If someone has trouble remembering names or items, allow the group to help. This game is particularly helpful if the group is comprised of people who do not know one another's names.

Beginnings' Cards

Acolyte

Usher

Choir

Worship Leader (Liturgist)

Organist

Pastor

Hidden Message

Find the hidden message by crossing out all of the Q's

Q Q W H E N Q W E Q Q

Q Q W O R S H I P Q Q

G O D Q Q S P E A K S

Q Q Q Q T O Q Q U S Q

Q Q A N D Q Q Q Q Q Q

H E A R S Q Q Q U S Q

Nametags

Make nametags for each person. Cut them apart, and mount each on a piece of construction paper or lightweight posterboard. Punch two holes in the top of the nametag, and tie an end of a twenty-four inch piece of yarn through each hole. Each week, the participants will color the symbol for the action of worship they are studying that week.

Session Two
We Gather to Worship

Main Idea

God's grace calls us together in community. God's people come together in praise to worship God.

Purpose

Participants will

- examine what we do as we gather in worship.
- learn about some of the symbols and tools of worship.
- explore the place of worship.

Bible in This Session

1. Psalm 95:1-7a (God's people are called to worship God, to sing unto God, and to praise God the Creator.)
2. Luke 2:41-52 (Jesus visited the Temple.)
3. Psalm 122:1 (I was glad when I was invited to God's house.)

Background for Teachers

People of faith need sacred spaces where they can feel the presence of God. These places provide comfort, help us make sense out of life, or help us experience anew the voice from the burning bush that shouts, "I AM WHO I AM."

Some of these sacred spaces are personal and private: a special corner in a house, a clearing in the woods, or a cabin on the seashore. For many Christians, however, the church sanctuary is a special place where they can experi-

ence God. In the church sanctuary, people of God gather week after week to renew their faith and to share in community with those who are sisters and brothers in Christ.

Children understand that the church sanctuary is somehow a "special place." They can sense the mystery of what a first grader called "the big room upstairs," and they know that something very different happens there.

Children also recognize that there are things in this special place that help us enter into worship. These tools help focus our attention on God, help guide our thoughts, and help us experience worship through all of our senses.

This session will introduce the sanctuary as the gathering place for worship. Participants will learn about the tools of worship, where these tools are located in the sanctuary, and how we use them during worship. They will begin to identify sacred places away from the church—in their homes or in their neighborhoods—that help them focus on God.

Preparing to Teach

1. Review Session One and any notes you made to help guide you through the preparation for this session.
2. Read Session Two.
3. Copy "Bulletin Insert 2" and collate it into the Sunday worship bulletin.

4. Find "This Is the Day" (No. 657) in *The United Methodist Hymnal*. If you are unfamiliar with the hymn, ask another adult to help you learn it.
5. Duplicate "Words for Worship" (p. 65) for each participant.
6. Gather the supplies needed for the activities.
7. Check the room for readiness and prepare the worship center.
8. Copy the "Letter to Parents" for Session Two for each child to take home after the session.
9. Copy "Tools for Worship Cards" (pp. 66-67). Separate the cards and mount each on a piece of construction paper or an index card.
10. Make photographs or gather pictures of the sanctuary in your church, of places in nature where people might feel God's presence, and of home worship centers. Look in magazines and books for pictures of other church sanctuaries and peaceful spots in nature.

Materials
1. Bibles
2. Pencils, markers, or crayons
3. Nametags
4. Worship items: another Bible, cross, candles, hymnal, offering plate, bulletin, paraments, water, bread, grape juice, candlelighter
5. Pictures of places where Christians worship
6. Two frames (made from black construction paper) for each person
7. Yellow or white tissue paper
8. Small pieces of tissue paper (various colors)
9. Glue
10. Ribbon
11. Scissors
12. Worship folders

THE SESSION PLAN

BEGINNING ACTIVITIES (5-10 minutes)
As the participants enter the room, invite them to find their nametag and to color in the second symbol of the church. Have them go to the area where you have displayed the worship aids. Distribute "Tools for Worship Cards" (one or more per person if possible).

Join the group at the table display of objects used in a worship service. Lift each object for the class to see. Ask the participants to identify the item and to state how it is used in a worship service. Ask those who have the appropriate cards (both the name and the description) to place them by the corresponding object on the table.

When all items have been identified, direct the children to sit in a circle for the next activity.

GROUP TIME (15-20 minutes)
Welcome the participants to the session, and ask them to name some of the things they remember about worship from last week's session. Give everyone an opportunity to respond.

Say, "We've already begun thinking about worship and the things we use to help us worship. All of these items are found in a place in our church called the sanctuary." Explain that the word sanctuary means "a safe place" or "a holy place," and it is where we go to worship God together.

Show the pictures of church sanctuaries to the class. Ask them to point out any of the tools of worship they identified earlier as they see them in the pictures. Explain that people can have other special places where they go to be close to God. Show the class the pictures of a beautiful spot in nature and the pictures of worship places in the home. Ask the participants to describe any items of worship in their own homes that help them feel closer to God.

Say, "Now we're going to read from the Bible about people coming together to worship. The first reading comes from the Book of Psalms." Read Psalm 95:1-7a. Ask the participants what they heard about how people come together for worship. Read next from Luke 2:41-52. Let the group respond by retelling the story in its own words. Have a time of silence, followed by a prayer thanking God for places of worship.

ACTIVITIES (20-30 minutes)
Make Stained-Glass Pictures
Give two paper frames, cut from black construction paper, to each person. Help each child glue a sheet of yellow or white tissue paper onto one of the frames. (If you are doing this as an intergenerational experience, match an adult with a child.) Trim the paper so that it does not extend beyond the edges of the frame. Then, ask the participants to cut, or tear, small pieces of tissue paper (using different colors) and glue them to the yellow or white window. The pieces can overlap. When the window is complete, glue the second black paper frame over the tissue paper window. Punch a hole near the top, and attach a yarn or ribbon loop. As the participants work, discuss how stained glass windows, photographs, and art help us think about God. Ask them to remember the pictures, photographs, or art in your church sanctuary.

Complete the Activity Sheet
Distribute the markers, pencils, or crayons. Let the participants complete the puzzle activity sheet, "Words for Worship." After they have found the words, help them say the words out loud. Encourage them to turn to the blank side of their activity sheet and draw one of the items named in the puzzle.

Write in Worship Folders
Ask one or two children to help you distribute the worship folders. Make sure each person has a blank piece of paper and a marker or pencil. Say: "Now is the time when we think about what we've learned today. You may write or draw about something you have learned. Remember, we've talked about worship tools and the place of worship. We've also read from the Bible about how people feel when they come to worship."

After the participants have finished this assignment, instruct them to place this page and their other activity sheet into their folders.

WORSHIP (5-10 minutes)
Invite the participants to bring their stained glass windows to the worship table. Sing "This Is the Day," using these motions as you sing:
"This is the day"
   (Stretch arms, palms up, out in front of you.)
"that the Lord has made"
   (Lift arms, palms up to the sky.)
"Let us rejoice"
   (Stretch out hands and place hands on the shoulders of the people next to you.)
"and be glad in it"
   (Clap in rhythm to the words.)

Ask the participants to form a circle, holding their stained glass windows in front of them. While they hold the windows, read Psalm 122:1. Lead a prayer, thanking God for places of worship that help us think about God and that bring us together with others who believe in God.

Distribute the "Letters to the Parents" for this session.

IF YOU HAVE MORE TIME

1. If you are meeting at a time when the sanctuary is not in use, take the class to the sanctuary. Let the participants use the "Tools for Worship Cards" to find and label the items. Sit silently in the pews at the front of the church. Ask the group to quietly look around, noticing the things that help people think about God. After a time of silence, lead the group in prayer, asking each person to name something he or she has seen in the sanctuary that helps him or her think of God.

2. Make a map of the church sanctuary. Using a large sheet of newsprint, or mural paper, draw the outline of the sanctuary. Label the front area where the choir and worship leaders sit and the doors where the people enter. Let the participants draw in the other things in the sanctuary. Ask them to write their names in the approximate spot on the map where they usually sit for worship.

3. Play the To My Right, To My Left Game. Sit in a circle. Lead each person in saying this sentence: "To my right and to my left are my worship friends. Today, my friends are _____ as they worship God." Then, he or she must name one thing people do in church. (Some things to suggest are: praying, singing, sleeping, smiling, humming, laughing, dancing, doodling, finding their money, reading.) No one can repeat what has already been said. Everyone in the circle acts out the activity named. Continue around the circle until all have had a turn.

Words For Worship

Find these words in the puzzle below.

ALTAR RAIL

BAPTISMAL FONT

CROSS

COMMUNION TABLE

PEW

PULPIT

ORGAN

BIBLE

```
B R C A L V S L R Y B R A E O R B A
E C O M M U N I O N T A B L E M A T
A N B Y D H L P T X U Q M I E B Q I
L F Z A F J P N R V Y C S O K G B P
T O G K O S W E A F P X T P L H D L
A R O Q A J T U W D E V K B R G B U
R G N I S C M S X T N F W L C S H P
R A M H R B L R W V U O G Q M W T R
A N D L Z B A P T I S M A L F O N T
I O U C K Y G Q A K Q P H X N D U D
L R V Z R J X F P Z J I Y O E V I M
G B F J N O E C Y Q B I B L E A Z T
L E P M Q U S X U M I E W T P L H V
S A G K O S W S D C Y V R N J F C U
```

Tools for Worship

Cross	This helps us remember Jesus' life, death, and resurrection.
Hymnal	This is a book of songs for singing.
Bulletin	This is a guide to use through the worship service.
Water	This is used for baptism.
Candle Lighter	An acolyte uses this to light the candles.

Tools for Worship

Bible	The Scripture lesson is read from this book.
Candles	These remind us that Jesus is the Light of the World.
Offering Plate	This is used to collect our money gifts to God, which help the church.
Paraments	These cloths are placed on the pulpit, the lectern, and the Communion table to tell us the seasons of the church year.
Communion Elements	These remind us of Jesus' Last Supper with his disciples.

Session Three
We Praise and Thank God

Main Idea

God's grace moves us to praise and gratitude. We praise and thank God.

Purpose

Participants will

• learn about the planned times in worship where we praise and thank God.

• become familiar with the Doxology as a song of praise used often in worship.

• consider the ways we praise and thank God through offerings.

Bible in This Session

Psalm 98:4-6 (Make a joyful noise to God.)

Background for Teachers

The next two sessions will focus on the second movement of worship: giving praise and thanks to God. While we may consider the first part of the service as the main place for praise and thanks, these elements are actually evident throughout our service of worship. We praise God through hymns, choruses, and songs. We praise God through prayers. We praise and thank God as we give of our tithes and our gifts.

Just as praise and thanks move through our worship, they also undergird our days. In the morning as we rise, we give thanks for the new day, and we praise God for the beauty and promise of that day. As we offer grace at meals, we praise and thank God for the good

gifts of food, health, and fellowship. At night as we prepare for bed, we praise God for God's goodness and thank God for the care and love felt throughout the day. As Christians, we live our lives in constant awe and praise for God's goodness and in constant thankfulness for the gifts we receive as the children of God.

In this the first of the two sessions on praise and thanks, we will look at the worship bulletin to help the children see the times of praise and thanks in our service of worship. The bulletin can be a valuable worship aid, particularly as children gain reading skills. And even beginning readers can recognize printed words and phrases used in the worship bulletin. The worship bulletin helps us know what to do, when to do it, and who leads us.

One act of praise we will be focusing on this week is the Doxology. A doxology is any prayer (sung or spoken) that praises the Trinity. The prayer we frequently refer to as the Doxology was written by Thomas Ken in 1674 and is usually sung to the tune of "Old 100th." This version of the Doxology is on page 95 of *The United Methodist Hymnal*. However, there are many other hymns that include a doxology. For these sessions use the words and tune that are used in your congregation's worship services.

As you teach the group words of praise and thanks and as you help them see those places in the worship service where they give praise and thanks, remember to include your own words and actions of praise and thanks. Children look to you, the adult, to see if your words match your actions. Hearing your praise and thanks and seeing you express that, not only with words but with your whole being, helps children grow in their ability to express awe, praise, and thanks to God.

Likewise, be open to the awe and praise expressed by children. As adventurers in the world with fewer experiences, they often tap more deeply into awe and praise because of the newness of their experience. Praise God that you may see anew God's wonderful works.

Preparing to Teach

1. Review any notes you made after Session Two regarding the participants' needs or your needs to make this session a better one.
2. Read Session Three.
3. Copy "Bulletin Insert 3" and collate into the Sunday worship bulletin.
4. Review the first stanza of the hymn "Come, Christians, Join to Sing" (No. 158 in *The United Methodist Hymnal*) and the version of the Doxology used in your congregation. Commonly used versions are found on pages 94 and 95 of *The United Methodist Hymnal*. Write the words to the first stanza of "Come, Christians, Join to Sing" on a piece of newsprint or posterboard. Display this near the worship center.
5. Duplicate "Praising God" (p. 72) for each person.
6. Gather the materials needed for this session.
7. Set up the worship center to reflect praise and thanks to God.
8. Collect worship bulletins for each person.
9. Copy the "Letter to Parents" for Session Three for each child to take home at the end of the session.

Materials

1. Bible
2. Pencils, markers, or crayons
3. Church bulletins (all from the same service)
4. Red felt-tipped markers, crayons, or color pencils
5. Nametags
6. Powdered tempera paint in two or three colors
7. White construction paper
8. Cotton swabs
9. Yarn or ribbon
10. Dowel sticks cut in ten-inch lengths
11. Water in a dishpan
12. Stapler or glue
13. Chalkboard and chalk or posterboard and felt-tipped markers
14. Writing paper
15. Worship folders

THE SESSION PLAN

BEGINNING ACTIVITIES (5-10 minutes)
Before the participants arrive, write the words BULLETIN, PRAISE, and THANKS on a chalkboard or posterboard. Welcome the participants. Invite them to find their nametags and to color in the symbol of a musical note. Say: "Today, we'll be talking about how we praise and thank God in our worship services."

Hand each person a worship bulletin. Point out the word BULLETIN written on the chalkboard, and have everyone say it aloud together. Explain that the bulletin is a paper guide for us to use in worship. By learning to read this paper, we can know when to sit and when to stand. We can know when to sing and when to pray. The bulletin helps us know when to speak and when to listen.

Say, "This week, we're going search our bulletin for the times we praise and thank God."

Point to the words PRAISE and THANKS. Ask someone to read these words for the group. Place the participants in pairs or trios. Pair those who can read with those who cannot. If you have no readers in your group, read through the bulletin aloud, and ask the children to raise their hands when they hear the words PRAISE or THANKS. Give each person a red felt-tipped marker, crayon, or color pencil. As they hear or see the words PRAISE or THANKS, ask them to circle the words in the bulletin. When all have finished, count the number of times the words PRAISE or THANKS are used.

GROUP TIME (15-20 minutes)

Invite the group to join you in your usual spot for group time. They should bring their bulletins. Remind the group that we are talking today about how we praise and thank God when we come together for worship. Say, "We can show thanks and praise to God with our voices and with our bodies. We're going to play a game of praise and thanks. I will say this phrase, 'All of us, all at once.' Then, I'll say something we're all going to do together to express praise and thanks to God. It might be something like, 'Shout Alleluia.' It could be, 'Fold our hands in prayer.' You'll need to listen carefully to what I say, and then do the action or say the words at the same time as everyone else."

Have the group place the bulletins in a safe place before starting the game. Play the All of Us, All at Once Game. Some suggestions include: Shout alleluia. Raise our hands to the sky. Jump up and down. Say: "Thank you God." Whisper: "Praise God." Turn in a circle. Shake hands with a neighbor. Clap our hands in praise. End with a quiet instruction, such as "Fold our hands in prayer."

Ask the group where it found praise and thanks in the Sunday bulletin. Explain that two of the things we do when we come together for worship are praise God for God's goodness and thank God for God's care. Tell the group that praise means saying something good about someone or something. Praise can involve giving thanks. Praise can be expressing the worth of someone or something. Talk about places where we praise and give thanks during worship and how they might appear in the bulletin. Include the following:

- Prelude—Music helps us prepare to worship God.
- Introit—We are called, by music and/or word to worship God.
- First Hymn—We praise God with instruments and song.
- Gloria Patri—We sing praise to God.
- Offering—With thanks, we give gifts to God.
- Doxology—We praise God.
- Anthem—As the choir sings, we are reminded of God's goodness and care.

Talk about the offering as a way of praising God. Define offering or gifts as the money we give to the church, the talents we use to serve God, the things we do to care for God's world, and the things we do for others to show God's love.

ACTIVITIES (20-30 minutes)
Make Praise Banners

Give each person a piece of white construction paper. Have them dip the paper in water, then sprinkle powdered tempera paint over the paper. Use cotton swabs to swirl the paint around. After they have created a pattern of color on their paper, have them write the phrase PRAISE GOD on their paper using felt-tipped markers. Staple the top of the banner around a dowel or use glue to attach the paper to the dowel. Then tie a piece of yarn around both ends of the dowel to make a hanger.

Complete the Activity Sheet

Hand each person a copy of "Praising God" (p. 72) and a marker or pencil. Show them how to unscramble the balloons to put the words of the Doxology in the correct order. Help those who need it to write the words of the phrases in the correct blanks. If you have an intergenerational group, pair a younger child with an adult or an older child. Sing the Doxology as the participants complete the activity sheets.

Write in Worship Folders

Ask one or two children to help you distribute the worship folders. Make sure each person has a blank piece of paper and a marker or pencil. Say: "Now is the time when we think about what we've learned today. You may write or draw about something you've learned. Remember, we've talked about the bulletin as a guide to help us in worship. We have talked about how we praise and thank God when we come together to worship. We give thanks and praise when we sing, when we say or sing the Doxology, and when we give offerings."

After the participants have finished this assignment, instruct them to place this page and their activity sheet into their folders.

WORSHIP (5-10 minutes)

Invite the group to gather around the worship table. Point out the poster with the words to the hymn "Come, Christians, Join to Sing." Sing the hymn. Then sing the hymn again using these movements as you sing:
"Come, Christians join to sing"
   (Join hands in a circle and walk to the left.)
"Alleluia Amen"
   (Stand in place and clap to the rhythm.)
"loud praise to Christ our King"
   (Join hands and walk to the right.)
"Alleluia Amen"
   (Stand in place and clap to the rhythm.)

"Let all, with heart and voice"
   (Join hands and walk forward to form a tight circle.)
"before his throne rejoice"
   (Walk backward to form a wide circle.)
"praise is his gracious choice"
   (With hands joined, lift arms in the air.)
"Alleluia Amen"
   (Stand in place and clap to the rhythm.)

Ask the children to sit in a circle and listen as you read Psalm 98:4-6. Lead the group in prayer, letting them offer words of prayer and praise.

Distribute the "Letters to the Parents" for this session.

IF YOU HAVE MORE TIME

1. Make a recording of the group singing the Doxology. Lead them in singing the Doxology three times. The first time through, ask the group to sing the Doxology in normal singing voices. The second time, lead the group in whispering the Doxology. The third time, ask the group to sing the Doxology as loudly as it can. Replay the tape.

2. Play the Ups and Downs of Worship Game. Using the bulletin, help the group find the places where they stand and where they sit. Those places where people stand are usually indicated by an asterisk in the bulletin. Call out parts of the worship service, such as "The Doxology," and see how quickly the participants can stand or sit as appropriate for the called part of the service.

3. Ask the person who develops the bulletin if he or she would use class drawings for the bulletin cover. If so, have the participants draw pictures that show praise and thanks to God. These can be used as bulletin covers for future worship services.

Praising God

Unscramble the balloons to put the words of the Doxology in the correct order. Write the phrases in the blanks to be able to read the Doxology correctly. When you have the phrases in the right order, color the balloons in colors that help you praise and thank God.

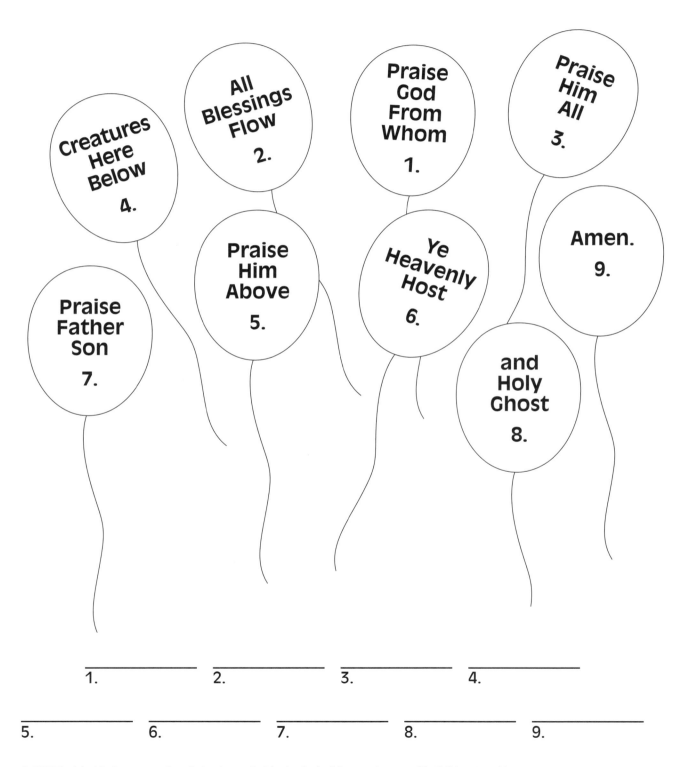

1. _____
2. _____
3. _____
4. _____

5. _____
6. _____
7. _____
8. _____
9. _____

Session Four
We Praise and Thank God

Main Idea

God's grace moves us to praise and gratitude. We praise and thank God.

Purpose

Participants will

• learn how music in worship helps us express our praise and thanks to God.

• become familiar with the *Gloria Patri* as a song of praise used often in worship.

• gain skills in using the hymnal as an important worship book.

Bible in This Session

1. Psalm 98:4-6 (It is good to praise God with song.)

2. Psalm 104:33-34 (I will praise God with song all my life.)

Background for Teachers

This is our second session that focuses on the second movement of worship: giving praise and thanks to God. One of the ways we have offered thanks and praise through the ages is through song and instrumental music. Have you ever heard someone say at the end of a worship service, "I just love that hymn! It touches my soul." Most people have hymns or songs of the church that speak to them in a deep way and make them want to praise and thank God. In this session participants will experience music as a way to express praise and thanks to God.

The book that guides us in our music is the hymnal. Children who are not yet proficient readers or counters have a difficult time with the hymnal. And, yet, they really want to use it during worship. Using one's hymnal is a sign of belonging to the church family. Children want and need to feel included. Holding the hymnal and singing from it help them know that they are a part of the family of God.

What children understand about the hymnal is that it is an important book to have in worship because nearly everyone uses one. In addition to the songs we sing, the hymnal contains statements that we read during the worship service. In this session we begin to help children use the hymnal. We give them hope that as they continue to grow, they will become more skilled in using the hymnal.

Preparing to Teach

1. Review any notes you made after Session Three regarding the participants' needs or your needs to make this session a better one.

2. Read Session Four.

3. Copy "Bulletin Insert 4" and collate it into the Sunday worship bulletin.

4. Review the first stanza of the hymn "Come, Christians, Join to Sing" (No. 158 in *The United Methodist Hymnal*) and the *Gloria Patri* (Nos. 70-71 in *The United Methodist Hymnal*). Display near the wor-

ship center the poster from last week with the words of "Come, Christians, Join to Sing."

5. Copy "*Gloria Patri*" (p. 77) for each participant.
6. Gather the materials needed for this session.
7. Cover the tables you will use for painting with plastic or newspapers, and prepare the paint.
8. Set up the worship center to reflect praise and thanks to God.
9. Copy the "Letter to Parents" for Session Four for each child to take home at the end of the session.

Materials

1. Bible
2. Pencils, markers, or crayons
3. Hymnals (one for each participant)
4. Nametags
5. Tape player or compact disc player
6. Tempera paint
7. Paintbrushes
8. Posterboard or white construction paper
9. Tape or compact disc of hymns or music heard in church (Consider the tape or compact disc that comes with Sunday school curriculum.)
10. Newspapers or plastic for covering tables
11. Writing paper
12. Worship folders

THE SESSION PLAN

BEGINNING ACTIVITIES (5-10 minutes)
Welcome the participants to this session. Invite them to find their nametags and to color in the second musical note.

Say: "Today, we'll continue our study of how we praise and thank God in worship. We'll be talking mostly about the music we use in wor-

ship and the hymns we sing." Explain that the group will write a song. Each person may add a word or phrase to the song. All of the words or phrases must praise God in some way. Write the words on posterboard or a chalkboard. Sing the song together. Add music by clapping your hands, snapping your fingers, patting your legs or arms, or tapping your toes. (A simple rhythm might be patting the knees twice, clapping hands twice, and snapping fingers twice.)

GROUP TIME (15-20 minutes)
Remind the group that we are talking today about how we praise and thank God when we come together for worship. Ask the participants to share their favorite songs. These do not necessarily have to be hymns. If the rest of the group knows the songs, you may want to sing them together. Ask: "Why is this your favorite?" "How does it make you feel?"

Ask: "Why do you think we sing songs when we come together at church? Is there a difference between some of the songs we have just listed and those we sing in worship?" Remind the group that the hymns and songs we use in church help us praise and thank God. Invite the participants to name their favorite church songs. Sing the ones you know.

Hand each person a hymnal. Help the group find the following in the hymnal:
• a hymn you use often in your congregation
• a prayer
• a creed
• a psalm or responsive reading
• the "Hymns for Children" index listing

Turn to a hymn. Ask the group if they notice something different about the way hymns are written. (After you finish one stanza go back to the top of the page to begin the next one.)

Pair older children or adults with younger children. Let each person show the other how to read and follow a hymn.

Read Psalm 104:33-34. Explain that many of the psalms are actually songs that were used in worship. Jesus knew many of these psalms and used them to worship God.

ACTIVITIES (20-30 minutes)
Paint to Music
Give each person a piece of paper and a paintbrush. Place paints so that they can be easily shared. Tell the group that you are going to play a tape of songs and hymns that praise God. They need to begin painting when the music begins. The colors they use and the speed of their brushstrokes are open to their interpretations of the song's "feel."

Complete the Activity Sheet
Give each person a copy of "Gloria Patri" (p. 77) and a felt-tipped marker or pencil. Explain that they will be searching for the words to the song. Tell the group that the title is in the Latin language, and it means "Glory to the Father." Show them how to locate the symbol in the puzzle and fill in the letter corresponding to each symbol to complete the words. Have a hymnal open to the Gloria Patri so that they may check their work. As the participants work on this activity, sing the song with them. You will probably be able to sing it several times. At first, the group may be slow to join in, but, as they hear the song repeated, it will become more familiar.

Write in Worship Folders
Ask one or two children to help you distribute the worship folders. Make sure each person has a blank piece of paper and a marker or pencil.

Say: "Now is the time when we think about what we've learned today. You may write or draw about something you've learned. Remem-ber, we've talked about the bulletin as a guide to help us in worship. We've talked about how we praise and thank God when we come together to worship. The hymnal contains hymns and words that we can use for praising and thanking God. One song we often use to sing our praises is the Gloria Patri."

As participants finish this assignment, instruct them to place this page and their activity sheet into their folders.

WORSHIP (5-10 minutes)
Invite the group to gather around the worship table. Sing, "Come, Christians, Join to Sing," using the movements they learned last week. Those movements are:
"Come, Christians, join to sing"
  (Join hands in a circle and walk to the left.)
"Alleluia Amen"
  (Stand in place and clap to the rhythm.)
"loud praise to Christ our King"
  (Join hands and walk to the right.)
"Alleluia Amen"
  (Stand in place and clap to the rhythm.)
"Let all, with heart and voice"
  (Join hands and walk forward to form a tight circle.)
"before his throne rejoice"
  (Walk backward to form a wide circle.)
"praise is his gracious choice"
  (With hands joined, lift arms in the air).
"Alleluia Amen"
  (Stand in place and clap to the rhythm.)

Read Psalm 98:4-6. Ask each person to name a song or hymn he or she enjoys singing as a way of praising and thanking God. Pray together, asking God to help each one remember to give praise and thanks every day.

Distribute the "Letters to the Parents" for this session.

IF YOU HAVE MORE TIME

1. Make praise instruments. To make a tambourine, have each person punch four to six holes (evenly spaced) around the edge of a sturdy plastic or paper plate. Use ribbon or yarn to tie a jingle bell at each hole. To make rhythm sticks, tape crepe-paper streamers to three-quarter-inch dowels of eight-inch lengths, or use unsharpened pencils. To make bottle shakers, place small shells, rocks, or buttons in empty, clean plastic bottles with lids. Secure the lids with tape. Decorate the shakers with permanent markers or by gluing pictures or stickers to the bottle. To create marching mittens, glue sandpaper (cut in a mitten shape) to pieces of posterboard (also shaped like mittens). Cut pieces of elastic to fit across the back of the posterboard. Staple the elastic in place. Slip hands through elastic, and then clap or slide.

2. If you meet at a time when there are no services in the sanctuary, ask the organist or a pianist in your church to meet with the class in the sanctuary. Ask them to play several hymns and songs of praise for the group. Sit where the choir sits during worship, and sing a hymn.

3. Make bookmarks for hymnals. Cut strips of construction paper. Provide stickers, markers, and crayons to decorate the bookmarks. Use clear contact paper to cover both sides of the bookmark. Let each person make several bookmarks. Place the bookmarks in your sanctuary hymnals.

4. Play a game of unscrambling a hymn. Choose a hymn familiar to the group. Use brown paper lunch bags. On each bag write a phrase from the hymn. Stuff each bag with paper and tape it shut so that it forms a ball (the writing must still be legible). Ask the group to form a circle. As music plays, have the participants toss the balls to one another. When the music stops, see how quickly those caught holding the balls can arrange themselves into the correct word order of the hymn.

Gloria Patri

One of the songs of praise and thanks that we use in worship is called the Gloria Patri. The title is in a language called Latin. The title means "Glory to the Father." Use the code to fill in the missing words, and you will be able to see all the words to this song. When you have filled in all of the words, decorate the border using markers or crayons.

Code

A	E	F	H	O	S	T	W
❑	▲	❄	◆	→	●	✚	✔

Session Five
We Pray

Main Idea

God's grace prompts our prayers. God's people speak and listen to God through prayer at church and in daily life.

Purpose

Participants will

- discover that prayer is talking with and listening to God.
- learn the Lord's Prayer.

Bible in This Session

Matthew 6:5-13 (Jesus teaches his disciples to pray.)

Background for Teachers

We now look at the third movement of worship: prayer. As a people of God coming together to worship, we respond to God's love, ask for God's guidance, and look to God for strength and help as we pray.

When one of the disciples asked Jesus to "teach us to pray" (Luke 11:1), Jesus spoke what has become known as the Lord's Prayer. Although we have come to use the prayer itself, it was really given as a guide to prayer. It contains many guidelines: seeking God's will for our lives, forgiveness, praise, and thanks for our blessings.

There are several different versions of the Lord's Prayer. (See pp. 894-896 in *The United*

Methodist Hymnal.) For these sessions, use the version that your congregation uses in worship.

Too many times we "say" a prayer that we have committed to memory and fail to think about the familiar words. Prayer can be a personal and a corporate response to God. As you work through the Lord's Prayer with the group, talk about the times we pray and how this prayer can be used during those times.

Preparing to Teach

1. Look over your notes from the previous session. Make adjustments based on the participants' involvement or lack of involvement in the activities of last week.
2. Read Session Five.
3. Copy "Bulletin Insert 5" and collate it into the Sunday worship bulletin.
4. Review the hymn "It's Me, It's Me, O Lord" (No. 352 in *The United Methodist Hymnal*). If you are unfamiliar with the hymn, ask another adult to help you learn it.
5. Duplicate "The Lord's Prayer" (p. 82) for each person.
6. Gather the materials needed for this session.
7. Prepare one or more wonder boxes. (See "Beginning Activities.")
8. Check the room for readiness and prepare the worship center.
9. Copy the "Letter to Parents" for Session Five for each child to take home after the session.

Materials

1. Bibles
2. Pencils, markers, or crayons
3. Nametags
4. A box or paper bag for holding wonder items
5. Small items for the wonder boxes (a flower, a feather, a rock, a small ball, a toy figure, a small stuffed animal, a shell, a bar of soap, a toothbrush, a comb, a leaf, and so forth.)
6. Bulletins from last Sunday's service
7. Green felt-tipped markers, crayons, or color pencils
8. Construction paper of different colors
9. Glue
10. Large sheets of paper
11. Envelopes for each person
12. Writing paper
13. Scissors
14. Worship folders

THE SESSION PLAN

BEGINNING ACTIVITIES (5-10 minutes)

As the participants enter the room, invite them to find their nametags and to color in the first set of praying hands. Have them move to the area where you have placed the wonder box. Use a box or a paper bag with an opening large enough for a hand to easily slip into but not large enough that the person can see what is in the box. Place several of the small items inside the box or the bag.

Say: "Inside this box are many things for which we can say thanks to God. I'll give each person a turn. You can reach into the box and get one thing. Before you pull it out of the box, try to guess what you have in your hand." Hold the box above the person's head but within easy reach. Let the first person pull out one item only. See if he or she can describe and name

the item. After the person pulls out an item, pray a thank-you prayer to God for that item. Continue the game until all of the items have been taken from the box.

GROUP TIME (15-20 minutes)

Welcome the participants to the session. Remind them that you have previously talked about how God's people gather for worship. You have talked about giving God praise and thanks in worship. Now, you will be talking about how God's people pray when they come together for worship.

Hand each person a bulletin and a green marker, crayon, or color pencil. Instruct everyone to look for the times when we pray during the worship service. Do this as a group, helping the participants to discover the times of prayer. See if they can find the Lord's Prayer in the service of worship.

Together, recite the Lord's Prayer. Say: "In the Bible we read about Jesus teaching the disciples to pray. I'm going to tell you about that and ask you to listen. Do the motions to this story with me as I tell it."

For each sentence, do the motions. Ask the group to repeat the sentence after you and do the same motions.

One day Jesus was teaching the people.
    (Hold up a finger, then spread both hands out in front of you as if pointing to lots of people.)
He began to teach them about prayer.
    (Place your hands together in prayer.)
Don't pray where everyone can see you.
    (Lift hands above you.)
But when you pray, go into your room, close the door, and pray like this:
    (Walk in place, make hand into a fist and pull toward you as if closing a door, then fold hands.)

Our Father in heaven,
   (Lift your hands and head.)
hallowed be your name.
    (Touch fingers to your mouth, then fold
    hands in prayer.)
Your kingdom come.
    (Stretch out hands, palms up in front of
    you, then pull toward you.)
Your will be done, on earth as it is in heaven.
    (Place hands palms down, and move them
    out and away from you, then point up.)
Give us this day our daily bread.
    (Bring hand to mouth in feeding motion.)
And forgive us our debts,
    (Bow heads.)
as we also have forgiven our debtors.
    (Point around the room.)
And do not bring us to the time of trial,
    (Shake your head back and forth.)
but rescue us from the evil one.
    (Hug yourself.)
Jesus taught these words to people long ago.
    (Point around the room.)
Jesus teaches us these words today.
    (Point to self.)

ACTIVITIES (20-30 minutes)
Write a Prayer
Divide the group into teams of three and four. Mix your groups so that you have writers and nonwriters together. Give each group a large piece of paper, several smaller pieces of paper, and a felt-tipped marker or crayon.

Say: "Often, when we pray at church, we ask people to say what has made them sad or frightened. We call these 'concerns.' We also ask them to tell us something that has made them glad. We call these 'joys.' Let's think about the joys or concerns we might have had this week." Help the group think about the things that concern them or the things that brought them joy. Be ready to share some examples.

Say: "Now, I want you to draw a picture of one of your joys or concerns. When everyone in your group has drawn his or her picture, glue the drawings to the large piece of paper. We'll use these to pray for one another in our time of worship."

Complete the Activity Sheet
Provide each person with a felt-tipped marker, pencil, or crayon, a sheet of paper, scissors, an envelope, and a copy of "The Lord's Prayer" (p. 82). Let them color the Lord's Prayer puzzle. When they have finished, ask them to cut the puzzle into pieces. Place these pieces in an envelope. Ask each person to think of someone who needs to hear the Lord's Prayer and to remember God's care. Be ready to name members of the congregation who would enjoy a note from someone. Let the participants write notes to these people. Put the notes with the puzzles inside the envelopes for delivery by mail or hand.

Write in Worship Folders
Distribute the worship folders. Make sure each person has a blank piece of paper and a marker or pencil. Say: "Now is the time when we think about what we've learned today. You may write or draw about something you've learned. Remember, we've talked about prayer today, particularly the Lord's Prayer."

As the participants finish, have them place this page and their activity sheet into their folders.

WORSHIP (5 to 10 minutes)
Invite the group to gather around the worship table. Sing ""It's Me, It's Me, O Lord" (No. 352 in *The United Methodist Hymnal*). Ask each group to display its pictures and to tell what joys and concerns were expressed today. After seeing all of the pictures and hearing the joys and concerns, pray for the group. End with the Lord's Prayer.

Distribute the "Letters to the Parents" for this session.

IF YOU HAVE MORE TIME

1. If you are meeting at a time when the sanctuary of your church is not in use, take the class to the sanctuary. Sit in the front pew and tell the group about the altar rail. Say: "This is an important place for praying. When we kneel at the altar rail, we feel close to God and place ourselves in a posture for talking to and listening to God." Invite the participants to kneel at the altar rail, fold their hands in prayer, and silently talk with God.

2. Make handprint prayer cards. Each person will need a white sheet of paper and a felt-tipped marker or crayon. Show them how to trace around their hands onto the paper. After they have traced their hand, ask them to write onto each finger and the thumb of their drawing the name of someone (or something) for whom they will pray.

3. Play the Prayer Posture Game. Explain that people use many ways of using their body during prayer. Illustrate the following:
   - standing but with bowed heads and folded hands
   - kneeling with bowed heads and folded hands
   - sitting with hands in lap and head bowed

   Make an index card for each posture. Say: "I'm going to draw one of these three cards and place it where we can't see it. Then, I'll count to three. On three, assume the prayer posture you think is on the index card. I'll turn over the card and we'll see how many guessed correctly." After each time, place the card back with the other two, shuffle them, and then draw another card.

The Lord's Prayer

Our Father in heaven,

hallowed be your name,

your kingdom come,

your will be done, on earth as in heaven.

Give us today our daily bread.

Forgive us our sins,

as we forgive those who sin against us.

Save us from the time of trial

and deliver us from evil.

For the kingdom, the power, and the glory are yours

now and for ever. Amen.

Session Six
We Pray

Main Idea
God's grace prompts our prayers. God's people speak and listen to God through prayer at church and in daily life.

Purpose
Participants will
- discover that there are many kinds of prayers that we pray.
- identify times when they can pray, not just at church but through the day at home.

Bible in This Session
1. Psalm 9:1-2 (God's people are to give thanks to God wholeheartedly.)
2. 1 Thessalonians 5:16-18 (God's people are encouraged to pray at all times.)

Background for Teachers
This is our second session on the third movement of worship: prayer. If we remember that worship is a dialogue, a conversation, a communion between God and God's people, we recognize that prayer, too, is a form of worship. It needs to be practiced by the gathered community during Sunday services and by individuals throughout each day. During this session you will help the group identify times for prayer, both in the worship services and at home.

Sometimes children question why we bow our heads when we pray or why some people kneel. Both the words and postures we use during prayer say something about our understanding of God and our relationship to God. We bow our heads to show honor and reverence to God. We kneel to show our obedience to God. We lift our hands to show our awe and wonder for God's love and care.

Children may also want to know if they have to be in a prayer posture or close their eyes to pray. Help the participants in your sessions know that they can pray in any way, at any time, and in any place. Children need to be assured that whenever they talk with God, God will hear and will listen to their prayers.

Before the session, think of some prayers you and your family use as you rise in the morning, as you prepare to eat, and as you go to bed at night. You may want to recite some of these prayers with the group. You might also want to keep a diary for one day, noting when and where you pray throughout the day. Talk with the group about your diary, helping them see how prayer is a part of our life as Christians.

Preparing to Teach
1. Look at your notes from the previous session. Make adjustments for this week.
2. Read Session Six.
3. Copy "Bulletin Insert 6" and collate it into the Sunday worship bulletin.
4. Review the hymn "It's Me, It's Me, O Lord" (No. 352 in The United Methodist Hymnal).

5. Copy "Word Search" (p. 86) for each participant.
6. Write one of the following words or phrases on four different pieces of posterboard: PRAISE and THANKS, CONFESSION and FORGIVENESS, PETITION, INTERCESSION.
7. Check the materials list and gather the supplies needed for the activities.
8. Duplicate "Prayer Treasure Hunt" (p. 87-88). Cut the prayers apart and hide them around the room before the children arrive.
9. Check the room for readiness and prepare the worship center.
10. Copy the "Letter to the Parents" for Session Six for each child to take home after the session.

Materials
1. Bibles
2. Pencils, felt-tipped markers, or crayons
3. Nametags
4. Posterboard
5. Drawing paper
6. Glue
7. Worship folders

THE SESSION PLAN

BEGINNING ACTIVITIES (5-10 minutes)
As the participants enter the room, invite them to find their nametags and to color in the second pair of praying hands. Say: "Hidden around this room are ten prayers. I need your help in finding them." Show the group what the prayers look like, and then let them search the room. When all of the prayers have been found, invite the group to bring them forward and to sit in a circle.

GROUP TIME (15-20 minutes)
Ask for volunteers to read the prayers aloud. After hearing each one, ask: "Would this be a prayer you would pray in the morning, at meals, or in the evening?" After all of the prayers have been read and you have decided when those prayers would be used, ask the participants to mention the times during the day when they pray at home.

Remind the group that you have previously talked about how God's people gather for worship. You have talked about giving God praise and thanks in worship. Last week, you talked about the Lord's Prayer. Say: "This week, we'll be talking about the different kinds of prayers we pray, the different ways we pray, and the different places we pray."

Lead the group in a discussion about different kinds of prayer. On posterboard, print these words, one to a sheet of paper, in letters large enough to be easily read:
• PRAISE and THANKS
• CONFESSION and FORGIVENESS
• PETITION
• INTERCESSION

Explain each as follows:
• Praise means saying, "God, you are great."
• Thanks means saying, "Thank you, God, for something or someone."
• Confession and forgiveness means saying, "God, I'm sorry. Please forgive me."
• Petition means saying, "God, please help me."
• Intercession means saying, "God, please be with granddaddy (or anyone else you are praying for) so he won't feel lonely."

Ask different people to say a sentence prayer. See if the group can guess which type of prayer they have used. Ask each person to commit to a special time and a special place for daily prayer.

ACTIVITIES (20-30 minutes)

Make Prayer Posters

Ask the participants to think about the four types of prayer. Show them the four poster-sheets that you used in the group time. Provide drawing paper, pencils, markers, and crayons. Ask that each person think about one kind of prayer he or she would like to pray.

Say: "Draw a picture of something or someone you want us to pray about. If you'd like, you can add a sentence that tells about the prayer. When you've finished your picture, glue it to the poster that shows what kind of prayer it is. When we come together for worship later in our session, we're going to use these posters to help us pray."

Complete the Activity Sheet

Provide markers, pencils, or crayons. Give each participant a copy of "Word Search" (p. 86). Encourage a younger child to work with an adult or an older child. Explain that all of the words in the puzzle are about prayer. Once finished with the puzzle, the participants can color the area around it.

Write in Worship Folders

Ask one or two children to help you distribute the worship folders. Make sure each person has a blank piece of paper and a marker or pencil. Say: "Now is the time when we think about what we've learned today. You may write or draw about something you've learned. Remember, we've talked today about the different types of prayers we say or sing when we come together for worship at church and when we worship at home. We've talked about the times we can pray in our homes or at school or as we do activities. We've talked about prayer postures and how we show God reverence when we pray."

As the participants finish this assignment, instruct them to place this page and their activity sheet into their folders.

WORSHIP (5-10 minutes)

Invite the children to gather around the worship table. Sing "It's Me, It's Me, O Lord" (No. 352 in *The United Methodist Hymnal*). Ask two children to read the Bible selections for the day. Have the first child read from Psalm 9:1-2. Discuss what it means to pray wholeheartedly. Ask the second child to read 1 Thessalonians 5:16-18. Ask the children to tell about the times and places they pray. Display the four posters of prayer. Ask those who are willing to tell the class about their prayer concern on the poster. Pray together, voicing the concerns seen in the drawings. End by saying the Lord's Prayer.

Distribute the "Letters to the Parents" for this session.

IF YOU HAVE MORE TIME

1. Make evening prayer door hangers. Use a half sheet of black or dark blue construction paper. Make a hole near the top of one end of the paper so that the hanger can slide over the doorknob. Have each person print a nighttime prayer on white paper. Glue this to the construction paper. Decorate around the prayer by drawing stars or by using self-stick stars.

2. Designate a prayer corner in the classroom. Using blocks, let the participants build a partial boundary around the corner, leaving room for people to come and go. Provide blankets or sheets, carpet squares, pictures of Jesus, natural world items (such as shells, feathers, rocks). Let the group decorate this corner in a way that helps them focus on God. Allow one participant at a time in the prayer corner for private prayer.

Word Search

Find these words in the puzzle below.

GRACE   BOW   PRAYERS

LORD'S PRAYER   BLESSING   DAILY

KNEEL   CONFESSION

THANKS   PRAISE

```
L O R D S P R A Y E R M N T
S T N S B B R Y N C K D P Q
S L F K X L N A Q I V Z B K
R C O N F E S S I O N L S V
E W D A C S G F J S H B L T
Y B A H L S M R X L E Q X I
A Z I T X I D B A V Z D Q Q
R D L E E N K C Z C N P F J
P L Y Q P G Y B O W E W K R
```

Prayer Treasure Hunt

Duplicate this page and cut the prayers apart.
Hide the prayers around the room for the treasure hunt.

God is great
God is good
Let us thank God
For our food.
Amen

As we rise
to greet the day
We give thanks
O God.
Amen

For health and strength
and daily food we give
you thanks O God.
Amen

Dear God: May we live today
knowing you have blessed us
and knowing we can be a
blessing to others.
Amen

Be present at our table Lord
Be here and everywhere adored
These mercies bless and grant that we
May feast in paradise with thee.
Amen
(John Cennick, 1741)

Gracious God
Bless this food that is
before us
And the hands that have
prepared it.
Amen

Prayer Treasure Hunt

Duplicate this page and cut the prayers apart.
Hide the prayers around the room for the treasure hunt.

Now I lay me down to sleep I pray the Lord my soul to keep Watch me safely through the night And wake me with the morning light. Amen	Dear God: Thank you for the moon so bright That shines on me all through the night Thank you for my little bed Where safely rests my little head Thank you for the stars above Thank you for your gracious love. Amen
O God: Help me make this day A day where I help others know your love. Amen	Praise God in the morning Praise God at the noontime Praise God in the nighttime Praise God the whole day through. Amen

Session Seven
We Proclaim God's Word

Main Idea

God's gives us God's Word. We listen for God's Word, and we proclaim God's Word to others.

Purpose

Participants will

- discover ways in which Scripture is used in worship.
- develop skills in using the Bible and responsive readings in worship.
- know what one Scripture says to them.

Bible in This Session

1. 1 Samuel 3:1-10 (God calls Samuel and Samuel listened to God.)
2. Psalm 23 (God will care for us.)
3. Luke 18:15-17 (Jesus includes children.)

Background for Teachers

We now look at the fourth movement of worship: proclamation. When we come together for worship, we come seeking to hear God's Word for us and God's call for us—individually and as a Christian community.

Throughout the history of the church, the reading of Scripture has been a critical part of worship. The Bible gives us the foundations of our faith and of our traditions.

When considering the order of worship, we initially think only of the Scripture readings as the place where the Bible is used in worship services. However, Scripture is present in almost every part of our order of worship. The responsive readings come from the Bible. Guidelines for prayer and the Lord's Prayer are found in the Bible. The hymns and anthems are often from the Bible.

Look at the bulletin from a worship service in your church. Look up the hymns and read the words. Examine the responses. Think about how each of these elements, based in Scripture, call us to life as disciples of Jesus Christ.

We hear God's call to us through our study of the Scripture, through prayer, and through others. We understand God's Word and God's call to us through the stories and verses in the Bible, through the examples of others, and through the teachings of home and church.

Preparing to Teach

1. Look over your notes from the previous session. Make adjustments based on your evaluation of last week's session.
2. Read Session Seven.
3. Copy "Bulletin Insert 7" and collate it into the Sunday worship bulletin.
4. Review the hymn "Tell Me the Stories of Jesus" (No. 277 in *The United Methodist Hymnal*). If you are unfamiliar with the hymn, ask another adult to help you.

5. Duplicate "Bible Scavenger Hunt" (p. 93) and "Proclaiming the Scripture" (p. 94) for each participant.
6. Check the materials list and gather the supplies needed for the activities.
7. Check the room for readiness and prepare the worship center.
8. Copy the "Letter to the Parents" for Session Seven for each child to take home after the session.

Materials

1. Bibles
2. Pencils, markers, or crayons
3. Nametags
4. Various translations of the Bible, Children's Bibles, Bible storybooks, and biblical pictures
5. Toilet paper cardboard tubes (one per person)
6. Material scraps
7. Rubber bands
8. Bulletins from last Sunday's service
9. Blue felt-tipped markers, crayons, or color pencils
10. Glue
11. Writing paper
12. Scissors
13. Worship folders

THE SESSION PLAN

BEGINNING ACTIVITIES (5-10 minutes)
As the participants enter the room, invite them to find their nametags and to color in the first Bible. Have them move into the area where you have displayed the various Bibles, Bible storybooks, and pictures of biblical stories. (You can often find excellent biblical pictures in the leaflets and packet books that come with Sunday school curriculum.)

Divide the group into teams of two or three. Give each person a copy of the "Bible Scavenger Hunt" (p. 93). Invite them to work with their teams to complete the scavenger hunt.

GROUP TIME (15-20 minutes)
Ask everyone to bring his or her scavenger hunt activity sheet and to join you in a circle. Briefly go over what the teams found as they explored the Bibles. Say: "An important activity we do every time we come together for worship is hearing God's Word through Bible readings. But there are other times in the service when we hear words from the Scriptures. The responsive readings are often from the Bible. Many of the hymns we sing and the anthems the choir sings come from the words of the Bible. Remember that the Lord's Prayer comes from the Bible too."

Give each person a Bible, a worship bulletin, and a blue felt-tipped marker, crayon, or color pencil. Ask the group to follow the order of worship with you. Instruct them to mark with their pen, crayon, or pencil anything in the order of worship that comes from the Bible.

Practice reading together one of the responsive readings. Help the participants look up the three passages of Scripture for today's session:
• 1 Samuel 3:1-10 (God calls to Samuel and Samuel listened to God.)
• Psalm 23 (God will care for us.)
• Luke 18:15-17 (Jesus includes children.)

Read these together, with the group following along in the Bible. If you have mostly younger children, show them where it is found in the Bible and then read, or tell, the story to them.

ACTIVITIES (20-30 minutes)
Complete the Activity Sheet
Provide markers, pencils, or crayons. Hand each person a copy of "Proclaiming the Scrip-

ture" (p. 94) and a Bible. Remind the group of the three Bible stories you read during the group time. Ask them to choose one of the readings and to draw a picture of what they heard or how the story made them feel.

Make Puppet Figures

Invite the participants to make a puppet of Samuel, or of a child who came to hear Jesus, by using a toilet paper cardboard tube. Show the group how to draw a face on the tube. Using the scraps of material, make clothes for the puppet and attach these with glue to the tube. Make a headdress using another piece of material, and secure it with a rubber band. Let each person retell the stories they heard from the Bible using the puppets.

Write in Worship Folders

Ask one or two children to help you distribute the worship folders. Make sure each person has a blank piece of paper and a marker or pencil. Say: "Now is the time when we think about what we've learned today. You may write or draw about something you've learned. Remember, we've talked today about the Bible. We've looked at several different kinds of Bibles, and we've found where we use Scripture in our worship services."

As the participants finish this assignment, instruct them to place this page and their activity sheet in their folders.

WORSHIP (5 to 10 minutes)

Invite the group to gather around the worship table. Ask those who are willing to tell the group about their Scripture drawing. Listen to each of them. Sing "Tell Me the Stories of Jesus" (No. 277 in *The United Methodist Hymnal*).

End with the following prayer.
Leader: The Bible tells us that God created the world.

Group: We thank you, God, for the Bible.
Leader: The Bible tells us stories about people who heard God call them.
Group: We thank you, God, for the Bible.
Leader: The Bible tells us that God will care for us.
Group: We thank you, God, for the Bible.
Leader: The Bible tells us that Jesus loved children.
Group: We thank you, God, for the Bible.
Leader: The Bible tells us that God loves us and that we are to love others.
Group: We thank you, God, for the Bible.
Leader: Amen.

Distribute the "Letters to the Parents" for this session.

IF YOU HAVE MORE TIME

1. If you are meeting at a time when the sanctuary is not in use, take the class to the sanctuary. Show the group the pulpit Bible and locate the pew Bibles. Allow two or three participants to lead the group in finding Scriptures in the pew Bibles and reading from the pulpit Bible. Look around the sanctuary to find other places where words from the Scripture might appear. (Many Communion tables have Scripture engraved on them. Often, stained glass windows have Scriptures written underneath the pictures.) Pray together, thanking God for the Bible and how it helps us know God.

2. Write cinquain poems about the Bible or about a familiar Bible story. (A cinquain is a five-line poem.) Follow this form:
   Title (one word)
   Descriptive words (two words)
   Action words (three words)
   Phrase (four words)
   Summary (one word)

For example:
Bible
Terrific Book
Listening, Reading, Praying
God's people discover God
Wonderful!

Write the poem together. Ask the participants to draw pictures that illustrate the poem. Ask if the class cinquain can be printed in the church newsletter.

3. Invite a person from your congregation to talk with the class about how he or she uses the Bible. Before your visitor arrives, help the group think of three to five questions it wants to ask your visitor. Questions might include: "What's your favorite Bible verse?" "How often do you read the Bible?" "Have you ever felt God's call to you because of something you read in the Bible?" "When did you get your first Bible?" List the questions and assign different people to ask each of them.

Bible Scavenger Hunt

Working with your team members, see what you can discover about Bible stories.

1. Find a picture of a Bible story you like. Write a sentence about that story or draw a picture of that story in this space.

2. Count the number of Bibles you can find in the room. Write the number in this space.

3. Write or draw a picture of one thing you think everyone should do when the Bible is being read.

4. Find a person in this room who can tell you the name of someone from the Bible who helps us know God. Write the name they tell you here.

Proclaiming the Scripture

One of the Scripture readings we heard today was_____ .

I found it on page _____ of the Bible.

This is a picture of what I heard in the Scripture reading.

Session Eight
We Proclaim God's Word

Main Idea

God's gives us God's Word. We listen for God's Word, and we proclaim God's Word to others.

Purpose

Participants will

- discover why we have sermons.
- explore ways of listening and responding to the sermon.
- begin to learn the Apostles Creed.

Bible in This Session

1. Colossians 1:28 (We are to proclaim Christ.)
2. Acts 3:11-26 (Peter preaches.)

Background for Teachers

This week we continue our study of the fourth movement of worship: proclamation. We will study the two methods of proclaiming God's Word—through the sermon and through our creeds, or statements of faith.

The Bible is the central emphasis in Christian worship. The written word (Scripture) and the spoken word (sermon) are primary ways through which Jesus Christ—the living Word—speaks to us. The sermon is a way of explaining the written word. The sermon opens the text of the Scripture, helping us answer the question: "What am I called to do as a child of God?"

The statements of faith, or creeds, of the church also help explain the Scriptures. These emphasize the central beliefs of our faith and put them together in a brief form. The Apostles' Creed is the creed most often used in Christian churches. However, it contains many confusing concepts for both children and adults. It is unnecessary to understand every word before saying the creeds.

Preparing to Teach

1. Look over your notes from the previous session. Make adjustments based on your evaluation of last week's session.
2. Read Session Eight.
3. Copy "Bulletin Insert 8" and collate it into the Sunday worship bulletin.
4. Review the hymn "Tell Me the Stories of Jesus" (No. 277 in *The United Methodist Hymnal*). If you are unfamiliar with the hymn, ask another adult to help you learn it.
5. Duplicate "The Bible Proclaims God's Word" (p. 98) for each participant.
6. Gather the supplies needed for the activities.
7. Cover the tables with mural paper.
8. Label the mural paper or newsprint with these titles: God Creates the World; Jesus Is Born; Jesus Is Crucified; Jesus Lives Again; God Is with Us; The Church All Around the World; God Forgives.
9. Check the room for readiness and prepare the worship center.
10. Copy the "Letters to the Parents" for Session Eight for each child to take home.

Materials

1. Bibles (one per person)
2. Pencils, markers, or crayons
3. Nametags
4. Paint
5. Paintbrushes
6. Mural paper or large sheets of newsprint
7. Paint smocks
8. Blank audiotape
9. Tape recorder
10. Writing paper
11. Worship folders

THE SESSION PLAN

BEGINNING ACTIVITIES (5-10 minutes)

As the participants enter the room, invite them to find their nametags and to color in the second Bible. Have them gather in the area where you have the tape player. Say: "Today, we're going to make a tape that tells some of the things we believe about God. Another word that means to tell is *proclaim*. I want each of you to think of one thing you know about God. Each of you may talk into the tape recorder and say the thing you thought of. When we've all had a turn, I'll rewind the tape and we'll listen to what we've said." Give the group time to think before you begin recording. If some are having trouble, give them suggestions. When everyone has something in mind, begin taping. Tell the group that it is okay to repeat something someone else has said.

GROUP TIME (15-20 minutes)

Play the tape. Explain that this activity is similar to what happens in our worship service every week: People come together to hear something about God. This time in worship is called the sermon. Ask for volunteers to complete the following statements: "When it's time for the sermon to start, I sometimes feel...."; "I think we

have the sermon because...."; "When I think about the sermon I wish...." Discuss the responses by allowing the participants freedom to share their feelings without judging what they say.

Explain that we have sermons because it helps us know more about God's message to us from the Scripture. The purpose of the sermon is to help us understand what the Bible tells about God, about God's love, and about how we are to live. Help the group state what they could do during worship to better listen to the sermon or better think about God. Remind them that it is okay to draw or write, to pray, to look up hymns, or to read in the Bible.

Say: "In worship we also often say creeds, or statements of belief. These help us, as a group, express that we believe in God, we believe in Jesus, and we believe in the Holy Spirit. In the creeds, we also say that we believe in the church, and we believe God is always there to listen to us and to forgive us when we do things we shouldn't."

Read aloud the Apostles Creed or the creed that is most often used in your congregation. (See Nos. 880-889 in *The United Methodist Hymnal*.) Tell the group that some words in the creed are difficult to understand. Point out the main ideas: belief in God, in Jesus, in the Holy Spirit, in the universal church, and in God's forgiveness. Tell them that it is okay for them to join the congregation in saying the creeds even if they do not understand every word. Practice saying the creed by saying a line and then having the group repeat it.

ACTIVITIES (20-30 minutes)
Paint a Mural
Explain that we can proclaim God's Word in many ways. Speaking, singing, and creating art are three of those ways. Explain that the class will now create a mural that tells, or proclaims, important things about God.

Each person needs to wear a smock while painting. Let each participant choose what he or she would like to illustrate:
• God Creates the World.
• Jesus Is Born.
• Jesus Is Crucified.
• Jesus Lives Again.
• God Is with Us.
• The Church All Around the World.
• God Forgives.

Encourage the group to paint anything that comes to mind about the chosen topic. Place the murals in a corner of the room or in the hall to dry. Later, display these in an area where others from the congregation can view them.

Complete the Activity Sheet
Give each person a copy of "The Bible Proclaims God's Word" (p. 98) and a Bible. Pair younger children with older children or adults. Let the pairs complete the activity sheet together. Instruct the older class members to show their younger partners how to find the verses in the Bible. Encourage them to check their work by looking up the verses in the Bible. (If your group does not include any readers, read the parts of the verses aloud, and let the group decide which beginning goes with which ending.)

Write in Worship Folders
Distribute the worship folders. Make sure each person has a blank piece of paper and a marker or pencil. Say: "Now is the time when we think about what we've learned today. You may write or draw about something you've learned.

Remember, we've talked today about the sermon and creeds. Both are ways of helping us know what the Scripture says about God and about the ways we are to live as a people of God.'"

As the participants finish this assignment, instruct them to place this page and their activity sheet into their folders.

WORSHIP (5 to 10 minutes)
Invite the group to gather around the worship table. Sing "Tell Me the Stories of Jesus" (No. 277 in *The United Methodist Hymnal*). Write a class creed, using the suggestions of the group. As the participants make belief statements, write these on a chalkboard or on newsprint. End the session by using your creed as a prayer.

Distribute the "Letters to the Parents" for this session.

IF YOU HAVE MORE TIME
1. Invite your pastor to visit the class. He or she should talk about the sermon and what he or she hopes to do each Sunday during the sermon. The class participants can tell the pastor things they would like to hear about in future sermons.

2. Make a videotape of the participants telling Bible stories they enjoy. Ask them what they think these stories are saying to the followers of Jesus. After making the tape, play it back so they can see how they have shared God's Word with others.

3. Invite the group to create a worship space using blocks of various sizes. Let them decorate this space with items from your classroom that they feel should go into the worship area. If you wish to do this in miniature, provide small interlocking blocks, and let the participants build models of places for worshiping God.

The Bible Proclaims God's Word

Complete the Bible verses. Draw a line connecting the first half of the Bible verse to the correct second half. When you have finished, check your answers by looking up these Bible verses.

John 15:17	**Proverbs 17:17**
Psalm 37:3	**1 Corinthians 13:4**
Psalm 23:1	**Luke 4:8**

Love one	the Lord
Trust in	at all times
The Lord	another
A friend loves	kind
Love is	Lord your God
Worship the	is my shepherd

Session Nine
We Proclaim God's Word

Main Idea

God's gives us God's Word. We listen for God's Word, and we proclaim God's Word to others.

Purpose

Participants will:
- learn the seasons of the Christian Year.
- identify ways we show the seasons of the year at church and at home.

Bible in This Session

1. Luke 1:39-56 (Mary prepares for Jesus' birth.)
2. Luke 2:1-20 (Jesus' birth)
3. Matthew 2:1-12 (The Magi visit Jesus.)
4. Matthew 3:13-17 (Jesus' baptism)
5. Matthew 27:27-50 (Jesus' death)
6. Matthew 28 (Jesus' resurrection)
7. Acts 2:1-4 (Pentecost)
8. Matthew 18:1-5 (Jesus teaches.)

Background for Teachers

When children walk into the sanctuary for worship, they likely notice the sights and sounds at first. Colors and symbols catch their eyes. They particularly notice when things change. When, for weeks, they have seen the color green throughout the sanctuary and they walk into the sanctuary the next Sunday and see that everything is purple, they wonder, "What is happening? Why have things changed?"

The church celebrates the changing seasons of

the year through the major events or themes in our Christian tradition. The church year gives focus to our proclamations of the Word. In each season we emphasize a particular part of the life of Christ. The Christian Year begins, not in January, but with Advent. The chart on page 103 summarizes the seasons of the Christian Year. Use this as you talk with the group about the church year. Remind the group that we celebrate the Christian Year when we gather for worship and when we are in our homes. This is another way we proclaim the message of Jesus and another way we proclaim how Jesus helps us to know God.

Although in this session we are focusing on how the church year helps us proclaim the Word of God as shown through the life and teachings of Jesus, we remember that the Word is proclaimed in all of Scripture, both Old and New Testaments.

Preparing to Teach

1. Look over your notes from the previous session. Make adjustments based on your evaluation of last week's session.
2. Read Session Nine.
3. Copy "Bulletin Insert 9" and collate it into the Sunday worship bulletin.
4. Review the hymn "Tell Me the Stories of Jesus" (No. 277 in *The United Methodist Hymnal*). If you are unfamiliar with the hymn, ask another adult to help you learn it.

5. Duplicate two sets of the "Church Year Cards" (p. 104). Cut the cards apart.
6. Copy the "Church Year Calendar" (p. 105) for each person.
7. Make arrangements to borrow stoles, or worship paraments, from the pastor for each of the seasons of the church year.
8. Collect church year seasonal items that could be found at church or at home.
9. Gather the supplies needed for the activities. (Make modeling dough if needed.)
10. Check the room for readiness and prepare the worship center.
11. Copy the "Letters to the Parents" for Session Nine for each child to take home after the session.

Materials
1. Bibles
2. Pencils, felt-tipped markers, or crayons
3. Nametags
4. Hymnals
5. Stoles or paraments for each of the church seasons
6. Advent wreath, crèche or white candle, star, cross, pictures of a butterfly, flame, triangle
7. Modeling dough
8. Writing paper
9. Worship folders
10. Calendar that includes the seasons of the church year

THE SESSION PLAN

BEGINNING ACTIVITIES (5-10 minutes)
Before the participants arrive, create a display that symbolizes the church year. Include the paraments or stoles that you have borrowed and other items you have collected, such as an Advent wreath, crèche, star, cross, butterfly, and candles. Have at least one item for each season of the church year. Pictures of any of the items can be substituted for the objects. If you do not have paraments or stoles, display instead pieces of fabric, or paper, that show the colors for each church season.

As the participants enter the room, invite them to find their nametags and to color in the third Bible. Have them move to the area where you have displayed the symbols and the colors of the church seasons.

Say: "One of the ways we proclaim the message of Jesus is by the way we celebrate important events from Jesus' life. In the church we have special days and seasons like we have the seasons of summer, fall, winter, and spring. The seasons we celebrate are called the seasons of the church year. Each season or day has a color and symbol that help us to remember particular parts of Jesus' life."

Give each person one of the "Church Year Cards" (p. 104). Help the group to identify the colors and symbols that go with a particular day or season. (Use the chart on page 103 if you need help guiding this activity.) As each item is identified, ask the person holding the card for that season to place it by the item. Point out that Epiphany is the last day of the Christmas season and that Pentecost is the last day of the season of Easter.

When all of the items have been correctly labeled, collect the cards, and invite the group to move to the place where you have group time.

GROUP TIME (15-20 minutes)
Remind the group that this is the third session that looks at how we proclaim the Word of God. Say: "I'm going to read you a story from the Bible. As soon as you know the church season based on that story, say the answer." Read the following Scripture in order. As the participants name the season or day, display the appropriate "Church Season Card" where the group can see it.

1. Luke 1:39-56 (Advent)
2. Luke 2:1-20 (Christmas Season)
3. Matthew 2:1-12 (Epiphany)
4. Matthew 3:13-17 (Season After the Epiphany)
5. Matthew 27:27-50 (Lent)
6. Matthew 28 (Easter Season)
7. Acts 2:1-4 (Pentecost)
8. Matthew 18:1-5 (Season After Pentecost)

When you have read all of the Scriptures and placed all of the cards in a row, tell the group that this is the order for the Christian Year. See if they can remember the colors and symbols that go with each season.

Give each person a hymnal. Ask for volunteers to name hymns they enjoy singing at different seasons in the church year. Help them find hymns for each season of the church year. If you wish, lead the group in singing one hymn for each season.

ACTIVITIES (20-30 minutes)
Make Symbols of the Church Year
Use modeling dough. Let the participants create one of the symbols of the church year.

You can make modeling dough by using the following recipe:
Mix together in a saucepan: 1 cup flour, ½ cup salt, 1 teaspoon cream of tartar, 1 cup water, 1 tablespoon oil, food coloring. Cook over medium heat until mixture pulls away from sides of saucepan to form a ball. Remove from heat. Knead 10-12 times and store in a plastic bag in the refrigerator.

Complete the Activity Sheet
Provide felt-tipped markers, pencils, or crayons. Give each person a copy of "Church Year Calendar" (p. 105). Have them color each section of the circle in the color that corresponds with the season of the church year. Ask them to draw a symbol for that season in the appropriate section.

Help the group identify the current season of the church year. Have them draw a circle around the name of the season. Using a calendar that shows the dates of this year's church seasons, help the participants find the church season that corresponds with their birthday this year. Have them draw a rectangle around the name of the season. Let the participants suggest other important days in their lives, and help them identify the season of the church year in which the event will occur.

Write in Worship Folders
Distribute the worship folders. Make sure each person has a blank piece of paper and a marker or pencil. Say: "Now is the time when we think about what we've learned today. You may write or draw about something you've learned. Remember, we've talked today about how we use colors and symbols to help us know the seasons of the church year. This is our way of marking time through the year. It reminds us of Jesus and of God. The Christian seasons help us to proclaim God's Word."

As the participants finish this assignment, instruct them to place this page and their activity sheet into their folders.

WORSHIP (5 to 10 minutes)
Invite the group to gather around the worship table. Sing "Tell Me the Stories of Jesus" (No. 277 in *The United Methodist Hymnal*). In your prayer time, ask the group to respond by naming the things that they are thankful for as you name each season of the Christian Year. End by praying: "God, help us to proclaim your love and care every day and in every season of every year. Amen."

Distribute the "Letters to the Parents" for this session.

IF YOU HAVE MORE TIME

1. Divide the group into teams of three or four. Assign each team a season of the church year and the corresponding Scripture. Ask the team to read the Scripture and to create pictures that illustrate what it says and how we celebrate that season in our churches.

2. If you are meeting at a time when the sanctuary is not in use, take the class to the sanctuary. Sit in the front pews, and see what you can find that signifies which season the church is currently celebrating.

3. Play a music game. Record music used at each season of the church year. Provide enough crepe paper streamers in the colors of the Christian Year so that each person has a complete set. Say: "I'm going to put on a tape of music. Listen carefully. When you know the season of the Christian Year when we would use this music, choose the correct color and wave your streamer in time to the music." Play the recording, and let the group respond by waving the streamers. If they have difficulty in matching the music and the color, give them hints as the music plays.

Season	Time	Colors	Symbol	What We Remember and Proclaim
Advent	Begins four Sundays before Christmas and continues until Christmas	Purple or Blue	Advent Wreath	Preparing for the coming of Christ
Christmas Season	Begins with Christmas Eve or Day and continues through the day of Epiphany (Jan. 6)	White and Gold	Manger	We praise and thank God for sending Jesus. On the day of Epiphany we remember the magi who came to see Jesus.
Season After the Epiphany (Ordinary Time)	Begins the day after the Epiphany and ends the day before Ash Wednesday	Green	Baptismal Font	Remembering the baptism of Jesus and the early ministry of Jesus
Lent	The fourty days, not counting Sundays, that begin on Ash Wednesday and end on Holy Saturday	Purple; no color or black for Good Friday	Cross	Remembering the last days of Jesus' life
Easter Season (Great Fifty Days)	The fifty days beginning at sunset of Easter Eve and continuing through the Day of Pentecost	White and gold; red for the Day of Pentecost	Butterfly	We celebrate the resurrection of Christ. On the Day of Pentecost we celebrate the gift of the Holy Spirit.
Season After Pentecost (Ordinary Time)	Begins the day after Pentecost and ends the day before the first Sunday of Advent	Green	Triangle	Proclaiming the teachings of Jesus about the Kingdom of God

Church Year Cards

Use these name cards to label the paraments and the symbols for the church year with the correct season.

Advent	**Christmas Season**
Epiphany	**Season After the Epiphany**
Lent	**Easter Season**
Pentecost	**Season After Pentecost**

Church Year Calendar

Each section of this circle represents a season of the church year. Color each section the color of its season.

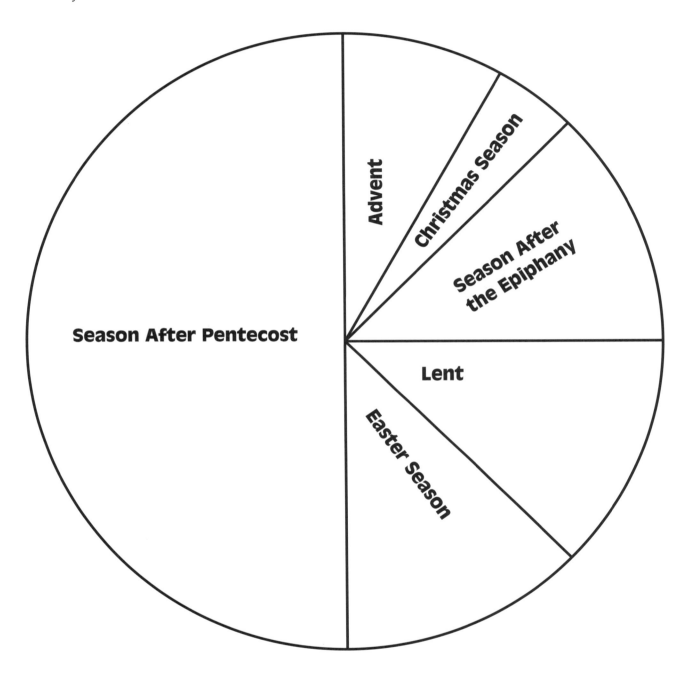

Session Ten

We Respond to God's Call

Main Idea

God's grace prompts us to respond to God's love. We hear and respond to God's call in our lives.

Purpose

Participants will

- identify the many ways we respond to God's call through our worship.
- explore the meaning of baptism.

Bible in This Session

1. Mark 1:9-11 (Jesus is baptized.)
2. Acts 8:12-13 (Believers are baptized.)
3. Acts 16:11-15 (Lydia is baptized.)

Background for Teachers

This week, we begin looking at the fifth movement in worship: responding. Having heard God's Word through Scripture, sermons, hymns, and other methods, God's people respond to what they have heard. There are many ways that we respond to God's call. In our worship services we respond in prayer and in statements of faith. We respond through song and through giving. We respond through the sacraments of baptism and Holy Communion.

Baptism and Holy Communion are the two sacraments celebrated in our church. They are both full of wonder and confusion for most children (and some adults). Through the sacraments we feel, taste, touch, and know God's grace.

Baptism is the sacrament that recognizes that we are children of God and members of the family of God. As a sacrament, baptism is God's gift to us. It is a means by which we receive God's grace. Faith is our response of God's gift of grace. Through our baptism we are called to ministry.

Water is the most powerful symbol of baptism, and it is used in all three methods of baptism: sprinkling (water is sprinkled onto the head), pouring (water is poured over the head), and immersion (a person is lowered into a pool of water). Water as it is used in baptism symbolizes cleansing, refreshment, growth, and the entrance into a new life.

Because we are wholly dependent upon God's grace, we believe that people of any age can be candidates for baptism. The United Methodist Church encourages Christian parents to present their children to the Lord for baptism at an early age. Whatever the age, baptism marks the beginning of a journey of discipleship. As baptized Christians we continue to grow in faith and to respond to God's love throughout our lives.

You may have children in your class who have not been baptized. Be sensitive to these students, making sure that the group understands that God's love extends to everyone.

Children Worship!

Preparing to Teach

1. Look over your notes from the previous session. Make adjustments based on your evaluation of last week's session.
2. Read Session Ten and the service for baptism in *The United Methodist Hymnal* (pp. 32-54).
3. Copy "Bulletin Insert 10" and collate it into the Sunday worship bulletin.
4. Review the hymns "This Little Light of Mine" (No. 585 in *The United Methodist Hymnal*) and "Here I Am, Lord" (No. 593 in *The United Methodist Hymnal*).
5. Duplicate "Symbol of Baptism" (p. 110) for each person.
6. Cover the tables with paper or plastic to set up for the water play.
7. Collect items that your church uses at baptism, including baptismal gowns, certificates, candles, and photographs of baptisms.
8. Gather the materials needed for this session.
9. Check the room for readiness and prepare the worship center.
10. Copy the "Letters to the Parents" for Session Ten.

Materials

1. Bibles (one per person)
2. Pencils, felt-tipped markers, or crayons
3. Nametags
4. Coffee filters, water, small margarine tubs, paint smocks, food coloring, plastic table cloth (or newspapers), medicine droppers
5. Baptismal gown, photographs of baptisms, baptismal certificate, baptismal candle
6. Illustrations from magazines, or old curriculum, showing baptism and the use of water
7. Scissors
8. Construction paper
9. Glue
10. String
11. Hole puncher
12. Writing paper
13. Worship folders

THE SESSION PLAN

BEGINNING ACTIVITIES (5-10 minutes)
As the participants enter the room, invite them to find their nametags and to color in the first chalice. Have them move to the tables covered with paper or plastic. Pour a small amount of water into three or four margarine tubs. Place several drops of food coloring in each tub and mix. Give each person a coffee filter. Show them how to take drops of water from the tubs with the medicine droppers and squirt a few drops on the filter. Let the participants experiment with making different patterns on their coffee filters. Help them notice how colors will blend and change.

Say: "When are the times in worship that we use water? What does water do for us?" Make a list of the answers.

GROUP TIME (15-20 minutes)
Ask the group to gather in a circle. Say: "We've talked about how people gather for worship, how we praise God in worship, how we pray to God, and how we hear God's Word. Today, we're going to talk about some of the things we do in worship to respond to God. Baptism is one way we respond to God's love."

Display the different pictures and items related to baptism. Ask the group if they have seen a baptism. Ask them to tell you what they remembered from the baptism. Talk about the items you have displayed and the pictures of baptism.

Tell the group that we find several stories about baptism in the Bible. Read or tell the story of Jesus' baptism (Mark 1:9-11). Then read or tell about the baptism of Lydia (Acts 16:11-15) and the baptism of Simon and the other believers (Acts 8:12-13).

Ask the group to describe the differences and similarities between the baptisms in the Bible and baptisms they have seen in their church.

Say: "Baptism is called a sacrament. A sacrament is something that helps us to know God and to feel God's presence. We celebrate two sacraments in our church, baptism and Holy Communion. These are both things that Jesus did and said that we should do. Baptism is the sacrament that says God loves us and says that we are a part of God's family. A minister puts water on the head of the person being baptized and says, 'I baptize you in the name of the Father, and of the Son, and of the Holy Spirit.' Water is necessary for us to live. The water used in baptism reminds us of new life. It also reminds us that God loves us and cares for us. When a person is baptized, everyone in the congregation promises to pray for that person and to help the person know that he or she is a member of God's family. Whenever a person is baptized, everyone in the congregation can remember that he or she is a member of God's family too."

ACTIVITIES (20-30 minutes)
Complete the Activity Sheet
Explain that a shell is a symbol of baptism. In some churches water from a shell is poured onto the head of the person being baptized. Some baptismal fonts (the place where the water is placed) are shaped like shells.

Provide felt-tipped markers or crayons and scissors. Give each person a copy of "Symbol of Baptism" (p. 110) to color. Ask the participants to cut out the shell and water droplets they have just colored. Punch holes in the shell. Using yarn or string, show the group how to tie the drops of water to the shell. Suggest that the participants take their shells home and hang them in a place where they can be reminded every day that they are a child of God.

Make a Water Collage
Provide paper, scissors, glue, crayons, pencils, and magazines with pictures that show water being used in a variety of ways (including baptism).

Let the group cut out the pictures from the magazines and glue them to paper. (Participants can also draw pictures that show how water is used.) Display the completed collages in an area where the other members of the congregation can view them.

Write in Worship Folders
Distribute the worship folders. Make sure each person has a blank piece of paper and a marker or pencil. Say: "Now is the time when we think about what we've learned today. You may write or draw about something you've learned. Remember, we've talked today about baptism. We've talked about water and its use in baptism and in our everyday life."

As the participants finish this assignment, instruct them to place this page and their activity sheet into their folders.

WORSHIP (5 to 10 minutes)
Invite everyone to gather around the worship table. Sing "This Little Light of Mine" (No. 585 in *The United Methodist Hymnal*) or "Here I Am, Lord" (No. 593 in *The United Methodist Hymnal*).

Lead the group in a responsive prayer, asking them to name uses for water (including baptism). After each person names something, respond: "Thank you, God, for water." Close the prayer by praying, "Thank you, God, for the people gathered here who are part of your family. Help us show your love and care to others in our homes, in our schools, in our communities. Amen."

Distribute the "Letters to the Parents" for this session.

IF YOU HAVE MORE TIME

1. If you meet at a time when the sanctuary is not in use, take the group to the sanctuary to see the baptismal font. If possible, arrange for your pastor to meet the group in the sanctuary. Have the pastor answer any questions the participants may have.

2. Play the Lemon Game. Have each person take a lemon from the basket (make sure you have enough lemons). Say: "I want you to study your lemon. Your lemon is unique. It's not like any other lemon that anyone else has. Like your lemon, each of you has been uniquely created by God and is loved by God."

   Give the group time to study the lemons and to decide what makes them unique. Collect the lemons from the participants. Mix the lemons together, and then pour them out on a table or the floor. Ask the participants to see if they can find their lemon. Most will be able to. Have them talk about what made their lemons distinct from the others. Remind the group that we are each loved by God and recognized by God.

3. If you have an intergenerational group, let the parents tell stories about their baptisms and the baptisms of their children. If you do not have an intergenerational group, invite someone who has recently been baptized or who has presented his or her child for baptism to talk with the group about the experience.

4. If the group includes adults, suggest that they read *By Water and the Spirit: Making Connections for Identity and Ministry* (Discipleship Resources, 1997) to learn more about the United Methodist understanding of baptism.

Symbol of Baptism

Color and cut out the shell and drops of water. Punch holes in the shell and drops of water where you find the ●. Put one piece of string through the hole at the top of the shell and three pieces through the hole at the bottom. Attach drops of water to the ends of the string. Hang this in your room at home to remind you of baptism.

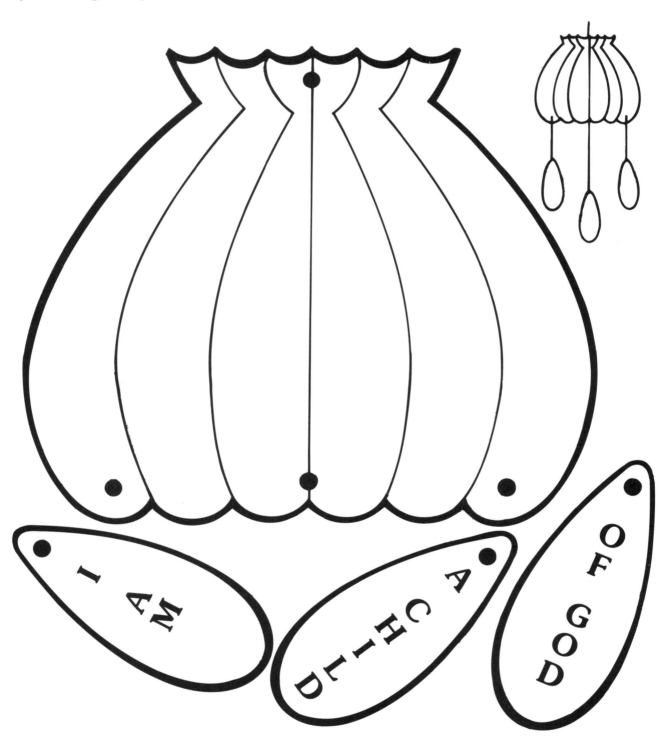

Drop 1: I AM

Drop 2: A CHILD

Drop 3: OF GOD

Session Eleven
We Respond to God's Call

Main Idea
God's grace prompts us to respond to God's love. We hear and respond to God's call in our lives.

Purpose
Participants will:
- hear the many ways we respond to God's call through our worship.
- discover how Communion is a response to God's call.

Bible in This Session
1. Exodus 12:1-20 (The story of the Passover)
2. Matthew 26:26-29, Mark 14:22-25, and Luke 22:12-20 (Accounts of the Last Supper)
3. 1 Corinthians 11:23-26 (The gathering of the early church to celebrate Communion)

Background for Teachers
This week, we continue our study of the fifth movement in worship: responding. Last week, we looked at the sacrament of baptism as one of the ways we respond to God. This week, we will focus on the sacrament of Holy Communion.

Confusion and misconceptions about the Lord's Supper are not unusual among young children. Remind them that the juice and bread are symbols—objects that help us think of another object, person, or time. In this case they are symbols of an important meal Jesus shared with his closest friends.

Children can relate to meals that are different (or important) and that signify a holiday or an event in someone's life. They can understand that we remember Jesus and the times he shared meals with his friends when we take part in Communion.

Churches celebrate Holy Communion in a variety of ways. In some congregations Communion is served in the pews and in other congregations people come to the altar rail to receive the sacrament. In some places Communion is served by intinction (dipping the bread into the cup) and in other places the bread and juice are prepared on trays. Make notes about the ways your church celebrates Holy Communion. Children need to know that there are different ways to celebrate it. Whatever way is used, remind them that the most important thing to remember during Communion is Jesus and God's love for each of us.

As children mature they will understand more about Holy Communion. It is not necessary for them to understand all of the meanings before participating. They realize they belong to God, and they know that Communion is a sign of belonging. When they come to the table to be included, they can remember Jesus and Jesus' teachings about God. By learning more about Communion, they grow in their appreciation for and understanding of this important time in worship.

Preparing to Teach

1. Look over your notes from the previous session. Make adjustments based on your evaluation of last week's session.
2. Read Session Eleven and the service for Holy Communion in *The United Methodist Hymnal* (pp. 6-31).
3. Copy "Bulletin Insert 11" and collate it into the Sunday worship bulletin.
4. Review the hymns "This Little Light of Mine" (No. 585 in *The United Methodist Hymnal*) and "Let Us Break Bread Together" (No. 618 in *The United Methodist Hymnal*). If you are unfamiliar with the hymns, ask another adult to help you learn them.
5. Duplicate "Symbols of Communion" (p. 116) and "Hidden Picture" (p. 115) for each person.
6. Gather the supplies needed.
7. Check the room for readiness and prepare the worship center.
8. Copy "Letter to the Parents" for Session Eleven for each child to take home after the session.

Materials

1. Bible
2. Pencils, felt-tipped markers, or crayons
3. Nametags
4. Tissue paper of various colors
5. Glue
6. Construction paper
7. Pictures showing Jesus eating with his friends
8. Pictures or photographs of congregations taking Communion
9. Paten and chalice
10. Grape juice and bread
11. Scissors
12. Writing paper
13. Worship folders

THE SESSION PLAN

BEGINNING ACTIVITIES (5-10 minutes)
As the participants enter the room, invite them to find their nametags and to color in the second chalice. Have them move to the table where the items used in Holy Communion are displayed. Include grape juice, bread, a chalice (or glasses and a tray), a paten (plate for the bread), pictures of Jesus eating with his disciples and illustrations, or photographs, of people taking Communion in church. Sample the foods used in Communion. Talk about the items that are used during the service of the Lord's Supper.

GROUP TIME (15-20 minutes)
Ask the group to gather in a circle. Say: "Today, we're going to talk about Holy Communion. Sometimes we call Holy Communion the Lord's Supper or the Eucharist. We use all of these titles to talk about the same thing. When we come together for worship in our church, one of the ways we respond to God's Word is through Holy Communion."

Review the story of the Last Supper by saying: "I'm going to help us remember a time when Jesus ate with his friends. As I tell the story, let's pretend we are together in the upper room eating with his friends." Tell the story of Matthew 26:26-29 in your own words.

Talk about the elements used in Communion. Remind the group that when we take Communion, juice and bread are always present. Explain the way(s) in which the Lord's Supper is celebrated in your congregation. Tell them where people go and what they do. Explain any details that could seem confusing or cause problems when the children take part in Communion.

Play a game to help the group remember Communion. Say: "Every time I mention a word that tells us something about Communion or says something about what we do in Communion, stand up. When I say a word not relating to Communion or tell about something we don't do during Communion, sit down."

Include words like: Communion, Last Supper, eating, bread, grapes, remember. Interject words and phrases like water, lemons, envelopes, and so forth. Praise the group for correct answers, but make sure not to embarrass anyone who stands or sits at the wrong time.

ACTIVITIES (20-30 minutes)
Make Communion Mosaics
Provide markers or crayons and scissors, tissue paper, and glue. Give each person a copy of "Symbols of Communion" (p. 116). Show the group how to spread glue on the illustrations of the chalice and the bread. Cut small pieces of tissue paper, and let them fall on the picture, covering the drawings.

When the drawings are covered with a mosaic of tissue paper, the chalice and bread should be cut out and glued to a piece of construction paper.

Complete the Activity Sheet
Provide felt-tipped markers or crayons. Give each person a copy of "Hidden Picture" (p. 115). Help them understand that they should color only portions of the picture to discover the hidden Communion elements. Explain that we call the bread and juice the "Communion elements." Once they have colored the elements, ask them to color the rest of the picture. As they work, talk about the bread and the juice at Communion. Answer questions that the group may have about the elements and about the service of Communion.

Write in Worship Folders
Ask one or two children to help you distribute the worship folders. Make sure each person has a blank piece of paper and a marker or pencil. Say: "Now is the time when we think about what we've learned today. You may write or draw about something you've learned. Remember, we've talked about Communion today. This is a way we respond to God's Word. When we have Communion at worship, we remember Jesus and we remember God's love for us."

As the participants finish this assignment, instruct them to place this page and their activity sheet into their folders.

WORSHIP (5 to 10 minutes)
Invite the group to gather around the worship table. Sing "This Little Light of Mine" or "Let Us Break Bread Together." Lead the group in a responsive prayer, asking them to name what they enjoy about eating with family or friends. Write their responses on posterboard. Pray together: "God, thank you for our time in worship when we eat together and remember Jesus. Thank you for the times we eat with friends. We enjoy those times because (*name the things that were listed*). Help us show your love and care to others in our homes, in our schools, in our communities. Amen."

Distribute the "Letters to the Parents" for this session.

IF YOU HAVE MORE TIME

1. Invite a Communion steward from your congregation to talk to the group. Ask the steward to bring the trays, cups, plates, and other items that are used for preparing Communion. Ask the steward to help you teach the group the manners of Communion in your congregation. Ask that the participants come to the altar and kneel as they would during worship. Have them act out receiving the bread and the juice and how they pray at the altar.

2. Design a Communion plate. Give each person a paper plate. Have everyone find Luke 22:19 and read it together. Instruct them to print "Do this in remembrance of me" on a card or a piece of construction paper. To decorate the plate, invite everyone to punch holes around the edges. Sew a length of yarn through the holes, and tie a bow at the top of the plate. Have each person paste the piece of paper on which he or she printed their verse in the center of the plate.

3. Bake bread, using frozen bread dough. Divide the bread among the participants and let them shape the bread into round, flat portions. Follow the directions on the package to bake the bread. Sit and eat the cooked bread together. Encourage the group to talk about what they think Jesus and his friends would have talked about when they ate together. Encourage participants to tell what they enjoy about eating with friends and family.

Hidden Picture

Color in each space marked with an "o" to find the Communion elements.

Symbols of Communion

We use the bread and cup to symbolize Holy Communion. Cover the symbols by gluing small pieces of tissue paper over them. Once you have covered the symbols, cut these out and glue them onto construction paper.

Session Twelve
We Are Sent into the World

Main Idea
God sends us into the world. From worship we enter the world to love God and our neighbors.

Purpose
Participants will:
- discover the parts of the worship service that send us into the world.
- identify ways we are sent into the world.
- learn how our offerings help spread God's message to the world.

Bible in This Session
Matthew 28:18-20 (The Great Commission)

Background for Teachers
We now look at the fifth movement of worship: the sending forth. When we come together to worship, we respond to God's love and ask for God's guidance. We look to God for strength and help as we pray. We hear God's Word through the Scripture, through the readings, and through the sermon. We respond to God's Word, and we are sent into the world to love and serve God and our neighbors.

In this session we focus on the sending actions of our worship. These include the giving of blessings, the commissioning of the people for particular tasks, the benediction and dismissal, and the fellowship and sharing that carries beyond the end of the service. We are sent to live as the people of God in our homes, in our schools, in our places of work, in our neighborhoods and communities, and in the world.

Included in this session is a closer look at our offerings, which is more than our money. We can offer many gifts, including our prayers, our presence, and our service. These offerings (including money) are both a response to that which God has given us and a way of extending the ministry of the congregation

Occasional special commissioning services occur in worship services. During the year children may see and participate in one of these services. Examples of these could range from a time for commissioning a person for short-term Christian service to the installation and dedication services for leaders in the church or teachers in the church school. You may want to recall some of those services and help the children remember what happened when these were celebrated.

Children will identify closely with the inviting element of our sending. If they enjoy their church and feel included, they are eager to invite friends to come with them. Help them see how this is a witness and a way of living out our commitment to Jesus.

Preparing to Teach

1. Look over your notes from the previous session. Are there activities you need to repeat? Is there anything you were unable to finish that you need to make time to do in this session?
2. Read Session Twelve.
3. Copy "Bulletin Insert 12" and collate it into the Sunday worship bulletin.
4. Review the hymns "Here I Am, Lord" (No. 593 in *The United Methodist Hymnal*) and "Go Now in Peace" (No. 665 in *The United Methodist Hymnal*).
5. Duplicate "A Child of God" (p. 122) for each participant and a single set of "Serving Game Cards" (p. 121).
6. Gather bulletins from the previous week's worship service.
7. Gather the materials needed for the activities.
8. Make a slit in the lids of some margarine tubs. Make the slits large enough for money to go through.
9. Check the room for readiness and prepare the worship center.
10. Copy "Letter to the Parents" for Session Twelve for each child to take home after the session.

Materials

1. Bibles
2. Pencils, felt-tipped markers, or crayons
3. Nametags
4. Sunday bulletins
5. Orange felt-tipped markers, crayons, or color pencils
6. Margarine tubs
7. Masking tape
8. Writing paper
9. Worship folders

THE SESSION PLAN

BEGINNING ACTIVITIES (5-10 minutes)
As the participants enter the room, invite them to find their nametags and to color in the heart. Move to an open area of the room and play the Serving Game. Sing the song: "This is the way we serve our God, serve our God, serve our God. This is the way we serve our God each and every day." (Use the tune of the folk song "So Early in the Morning.")

Play the Serving Game by having a participant act out a way of serving God at home, at school, in the community, or in the world. The rest of the class should guess what has been acted out. Sing the song again, and then let another person act out a way of serving. Each participant should have a turn. If you feel your group needs suggestions, use the "Serving Game Cards" (p. 121). Let a participant draw a card and then act it out for the others to guess.

GROUP TIME (15-20 minutes)
Remind the group that you have previously talked about how God's people gather for worship. You have talked about giving God praise and thanks in worship. You have talked about prayer and hearing God's Word. You have talked about responding to God's Word. Say: "Today, we'll look at how we're sent from worship into the world to live as God would want us to live so that others will come to know God."

Give each person a bulletin and an orange marker. Together, locate the sending portion of the worship service. Underline all of the things in the bulletin that tell us we are sent into the world to be a witness of God and to serve the world. Help the group see that the sending happens not just at the end of the service but at other places as well: in the words of the songs we sing, in the giving of our offerings, and in our fellowship times at the beginning, during, and following the worship service.

Read Matthew 28:18-20. Ask the group to repeat the following phrases after you say them (say the phrases with lots of energy and feeling):
Jesus said, "Go!"
Go to all the world!
Baptize!
Teach!
I will be with you!

Make a chart showing how the money you give in church is used to serve others by listing the ideas of the group on newsprint or poster-board. Add your own suggestions.

ACTIVITIES (20-30 minutes)
Make Offering Containers
Give each person a margarine tub. Provide masking tape and felt-tipped markers or crayons. Say: "Today, we're going to make containers for you to take home. Put the money you want to give in church in this container. When the container is full, you can cut off the top and bring the money to the church. The money we give in church helps us serve others in the world. The money we give in church can be for people who are hungry, for people in other countries where there is war, for Sunday school supplies and items we need at church, for people who have no homes, for people who work in our church—our organist, our pastor, and our custodian."

Show the class how to tear strips of masking tape off the roll and how to wrap the tape around the containers. Keep placing strips of tape on the container until it is completely covered. Use the markers or crayons to color the tape. Ask them to print "CHURCH MONEY" on the top.

Complete the Activity Sheet
Provide felt-tipped markers, pencils, or crayons for each person. They will need to write their names at the top of the page and then circle all of the words that describe them. They can add words to the sheet. At the bottom of the sheet, they are instructed to draw a self portrait. As the children work, talk about how we serve God through our gifts and talents.

Write in Worship Folders
Ask one or two children to help you distribute the worship folders. Make sure each person has a blank piece of paper and a marker or pencil. Say: "Now is the time when we think about what we've learned today. You may write or draw about something you've learned. Remember, we've talked today about how we are sent into the world as disciples of Jesus. We talked about the ways we can serve—by giving our money, by giving our time for service projects, by telling others about our church, and by letting people know we miss them when they are not here."

As the participants finish this assignment, instruct them to place this page and their activity sheet in their folders.

WORSHIP (5 to 10 minutes)
Invite the group to gather around the worship table. Sing "Here I Am Lord" or "Go Now in Peace." Ask each person to stand, one by one. Go around the circle and place your hands on the head of each one. Say, "God bless (name). We thank you for (his/her) presence here. We thank you for the ways (name) is able to serve you. Amen." End your worship time by saying the Lord's Prayer.

Distribute the "Letters to the Parents" for this session.

IF YOU HAVE MORE TIME

1. Lead a church scavenger hunt. Divide the group into teams of three or four. Give each team a checklist. Ask the teams to see how many of the following items they can find. Explain that each item represents a way we serve. You may want to limit the hunt to certain rooms. Suggested items include:
   - names or letters from missionaries
   - food collection boxes
   - prayer lists
   - offering plates
   - sign-up sheets for service projects
   - pictures of visitors or badges to give to visitors

   Limit the time for the search. When all of the teams have returned, compare what was discovered about how your congregation serves the world.

2. Obtain a list of people in the congregation who have not been at church for several weeks. Write "We Miss You" notes to these people. Depending on the size of your congregation, you may want to focus on one or two Sunday school classes for names. Encourage the group to draw pictures on the notes and to personalize them if they know the person they are writing.

3. Make coin rubbings. Place coins on a table. Let the group examine them. Give each person a piece of typing paper, a peeled crayon, and several coins. Have the participants put their papers over the coins and rub the side of the crayon across the coins. The imprint of the coins will appear on the paper. Encourage the group to talk about the money given to the church. Talk about who the money serves. Make a list and help the group think of ways the money is used, both for the congregation and in service to the community and to the world.

Serving Game Cards

Putting money in the offering plate	**Singing songs about God**	**Helping feed the hungry**
Giving clothes to those who need them	**Praying for others**	**Inviting people to church**
Writing notes to people	**Visiting the sick**	**Mowing the church yard**
Reading the Bible	**Bringing friends to church**	**Calling people who are lonely**
Recycling	**Caring for the earth**	

A Child of God

_____(NAME) *was created by God with these gifts and talents*

(Circle all the words that describe you)

QUIET	PLAYS A MUSICAL INSTRUMENT	STRONG
CURIOUS	KIND	READER
WELCOMES PEOPLE	BALLPLAYER	LIKES ANIMALS
FRIENDLY	HELPS IN WORSHIP	BIG SISTER OR BROTHER
CHEERFUL	BIBLE READER	LIKES MATH
LIKES MUSIC	LITTLE BROTHER OR SISTER	PATIENT
SHARES WITH OTHERS	GREAT SMILE	LIKES PLANTS
HELPS WILLINGLY	HAPPY	GENTLE

Draw a picture of yourself—a gifted and talented follower of Jesus.

Session Thirteen
We Worship God!

Main Idea

God's grace leads us to worship God. We worship God.

Purpose

Participants will:
- review all of the movements of worship.
- celebrate the completion of this study.
- celebrate that they are important participants in worship.

Bible in This Session

Psalm 95:6-7 (A call to worship)

Background for Teachers

This is the final session of *Children Worship!* As you prepare for this week's session, think back over the entire study. What have you enjoyed most? What have you learned about worship—from the material and from those with whom you have been working? What has been difficult to teach and difficult for the participants to understand? What suggestions do you have for the next time your church offers these sessions? You may wish to use this session as a time for review. Choose games, hymns, and activities from previous sessions that the group enjoyed. Include activities that you did not have time to do. Celebrate the learning time you have had together.

As you think through the entire study, have the participants been able to
- know that they are important members of the people of God who gather for worship?
- see ways of worshiping God at church and at home?
- recognize some of the responses and prayers used in worship?
- see the symbols and signs of worship in our sanctuaries and in our homes?
- realize that through worship we listen to God?
- understand that we leave worship asking ourselves how we can serve others because we love God?

At the conclusion of this course, you may wish to plan ways for those who have been involved in these sessions to take a leadership role in an upcoming worship service. Talk with your pastor. Work together on a recognition service that could be a part of a worship service. Choose activities for this session that will allow those in the class to contribute to the worship service.

Please note the evaluation on the last page of this book. The General Board of Disipleship is very interested in your feedback. The comments you provide will help us to plan and improve resources.

Preparing to Teach

1. Look over your notes from the previous session. This will be the final session. Are there activities you wish to repeat?
2. Read Session Thirteen.
3. Copy "Bulletin Insert 13" and collate it into the Sunday worship bulletin.
4. Review the hymns you have learned. Choose to sing two or three hymns that you and the participants have especially enjoyed.
5. Duplicate "Bible Verse Chain" (p. 127) for each person.
6. If you are preparing for participation in a worship service, contact the pastor for an order of worship and mark the places where the group will lead.
7. Make two signs. One should say AGREE. The other should say DISAGREE. Place one sign on one wall and the other sign on the opposite wall.
8. Gather any artwork or projects done by participants and place these in paper bags so that they can be easily distributed when the session ends.
9. Gather the supplies needed.
10. Check the room for readiness and prepare the worship center.
11. Copy the "Letters to the Parents" for Session Thirteen for each child to take home after the session.

Materials

1. Bibles
2. Pencils, markers, or crayons
3. Nametags
4. Hymnals
5. Agree/disagree signs
6. Posterboard
7. Drawing and writing paper
8. Worship folders

THE SESSION PLAN

BEGINNING ACTIVITIES (5-10 minutes)
As the participants enter the room, invite them to find their nametags and to color in the cross. Have them gather in the middle of the room to play the AGREE/DISAGREE game. Show them the two signs posted on opposite walls. Say: "We're going to play a game where you have to decide if you agree or disagree with what I say about worship. I'll read a sentence. You decide whether you agree or disagree with that sentence, then move to the side of the room that says 'agree' if you think the sentence is correct. If you think it's wrong, move to the side of the room that says 'disagree.'" Use the following statements:

- Children do not belong in worship.
- We use the color blue at Advent.
- Candles remind us that Jesus is the light of the world.
- Boys and girls are too young to be a leader in worship.
- Only older people are welcome to take Communion.
- When we sing hymns, we are praising God.
- We cannot laugh or smile in worship.

After each statement, ask one or two to say why they chose agree or disagree. Add more questions that are suitable for your group.

GROUP TIME (15-20 minutes)
Remind the group that this is our last session. Ask the group to name the things that they have most enjoyed about the sessions. Use a markerboard, chalkboard, or posterboard to record responses. After each suggestion clap hands or shout hooray as a way of celebrating what they have enjoyed.

Review with the group what you have learned about worship together. Go around the circle, and let each person complete the phrase, "Worship is...." After each person completes the sentence, lead the group in responding, "Thanks be to God." Write each sentence on a sheet of paper and give it to the person who said it. Tell them that they can use their sentences as a basis for pictures they will draw later, which may be used for a bulletin cover. Be ready to make suggestions if there are those who cannot think of anything. More than one person can say the same thing.

Turn in your Bible to Psalm 95:6-7. Ask the group to listen carefully as you read the verses. Then say, "Now we're going to repeat these verses several times. I'll ask you to repeat the verses in a certain way after me. Listen carefully so you'll know how to say the verses." Use two or three of the following suggestions:
• Sing the verses.
• Shout the verses.
• Pray the verses.
• Say the verses in a happy voice.
• Say the verses is a sad voice.
• Say the verses in a whisper voice.

ACTIVITIES (20-30 minutes)
Design a Bulletin Cover or Insert
This activity assumes that you have already secured permission from the person in charge of producing the church bulletin.

Provide paper and felt-tipped markers. Remind each participant to use his or her sentence about worship from the group time. Ask each person to draw a picture that shows what he or she has learned about worship. Tell them that they will need to leave these pictures with you so that you can give them to the church office. Some class members may want to do two pictures, one to leave with you and one that they can take home.

Complete the Activity Sheet
Provide markers, pencils, or crayons for each person. Show the group how to follow the chain and write each letter in the spaces provided on the chain. When all have finished, read the verse together. Ask the group what it means when Jesus says, "Let the children come...." Talk about the ways your church includes children in worship as leaders and as participants.

Write in Worship Folders
Ask one or two children to help you distribute the worship folders. Make sure each person has a blank piece of paper and a marker or pencil. Say: "Now is the time when we think about what we've learned today. You may write or draw about something you've learned. Remember, today is our last session. You may want to draw or write something about what we've done today or you may want to write about how you feel about the time we've spent learning together."

As the participants finish this assignment, instruct them to place this page and their activity sheet into their folders. Put the folders in a place where all class members can see them and will remember to take them home at the end of the session.

WORSHIP (5 to 10 minutes)
Invite the group to gather around the worship table. Ask them to suggest hymns that they would like to sing. Name some that you have learned together to help them remember the hymns from past sessions. Pray a prayer of thanks, calling each person by name and thanking God for his or her participation in the sessions.

Distribute the final "Letter to the Parents," the worship folders, and any other artwork or writing projects the participants have done over the past sessions.

IF YOU HAVE MORE TIME

1. Write a Haiku about worship. Haiku is a three-line poem. The first line has five syllables. The second line has seven syllables. The third line has five syllables. An example is:

Church

Church is a fun place.
We sing and praise God at church.
God listens to us.

As a group, write a poem, and then ask each person to illustrate the Haiku. Or let each person write a poem and then illustrate it. Encourage them to write the poems about worship, including anything you have learned together in these sessions. Participants may want to pick one of the actions of worship—gathering, thanking and praising, praying, proclaiming, responding, and sending—as a focus for their Haikus.

2. Prepare to participate in a worship service. Recruit volunteers to help as an usher, as a greeter, as an acolyte, or as a leader of the litany or a prayer. If you are meeting at a time when the sanctuary is not in use, go to the sanctuary. Let the volunteers practice the parts they will have in the worship service. Have those who have not volunteered play the part of the congregation, asking them to find a place to sit and to follow the directions of the worship leaders.

3. Make a cloth for the altar table, the pulpit, or lectern. Use fabric paint and a piece of white cloth. Paint the symbols that represent the seasons of the church year on the cloth. If you will be participating in an upcoming worship service, present the cloth to the congregation in that worship service.

4. Write a litany, using the phrase, "Worship is..." with the response of the people being, "Thanks be to God." If you will be leading in a worship service, use this litany in the service.

Bible Verse Chain

Follow the chain of circles to find the Bible verse.
Write the letter in each circle in the correct space.

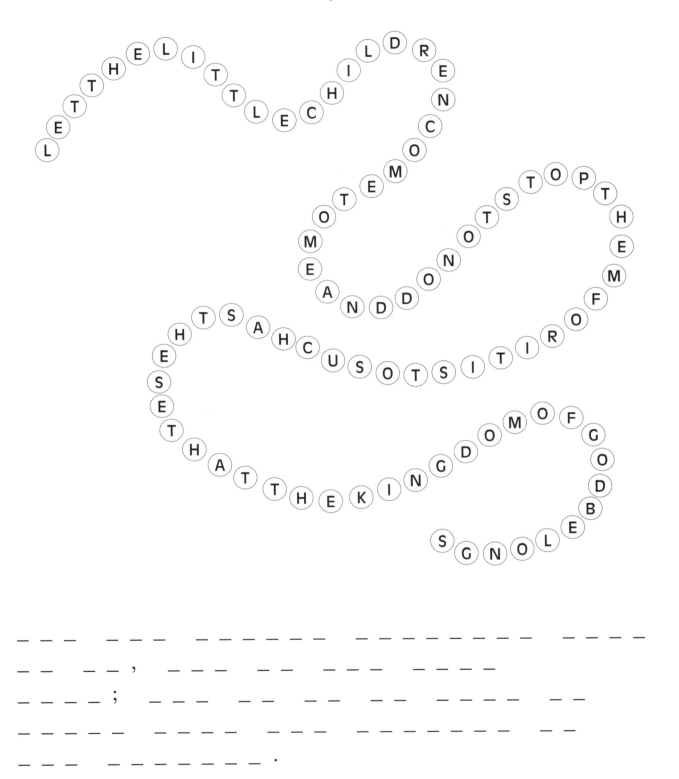

_ _ _   _ _ _   _ _ _ _   _ _ _ _ _ _   _ _ _

_ _   _ _ ,   _ _ _   _ _   _ _ _   _ _ _   _

_ _ _ _ ;   _ _ _   _ _   _ _   _ _ _   _ _

_ _ _ _ _   _ _ _ _ _ _   _ _

_ _ _   _ _ _ _ _ _ _ .

Evaluation

Please take a few moments to help us evaluate this resource.

Rank these statements
1= Strongly agree
2= Agree
3= Disagree
4= Strongly disagree

☐ This resource was easy to use.
☐ The people who participated in the study will find worship more meaningful.
☐ Members of the congregation believe it is important for children to participate in the worship service.
☐ More children will attend worship because of participation in *Children Worship!*
☐ Parents understand the importance of children being in worship.

Rank the components of this resource
1= Great! We couldn't have done without it.
2= OK. We modified it to meet our needs.
3= We didn't use it but wish we had.
4= A waste of paper.

☐ Checklist for planning
☐ Teacher training model
☐ Chart with worship suggestions
☐ Letters to parents
☐ Bulletin inserts
☐ Session plans
☐ Reproducible activity sheets

Tell us a little about yourself

Church _____
City _____ State _____

Who participated in *Children Worship!*?
(Check all that apply.)
☐ An intergenerational church-wide study
☐ With children only (indicate the ages _____)
☐ With children and their parents (indicate ages of children)
☐ Other

_____

When did you have the sessions
☐ During the week
☐ On Sunday morning during Sunday school
☐ On Sunday morning during the worship service
☐ A weekend retreat
☐ Sunday evenings
☐ Other (please describe)

_____

Please duplicate this evaluation, add any additional comments on the back of the page, and send the evaluation to:

Acquisitions Editor,
    Family and Life Span Ministries
General Board of Discipleship
P.O. Box 840
Nashville, TN 37212

Name _____ Mailing Address _____

City _____ State _____ Zip _____

E-Mail (optional) _____